Heist

Heist

The Inside Story of Scotland's Most Notorious Raids

Paul Smith

BIRLINN

First published in 2014 by
Birlinn Limited
West Newington House
10 Newington Road
Edinburgh
EH9 1QS

www.birlinn.co.uk

ISBN: 978 1 78027 198 9

British Library Cataloguing-in-Publication Data
A catalogue record for this book is available from the British Library

Typeset by Iolaire Typesetting, Newtonmore
Printed and bound by Gutenberg Press, Malta

To Coral, Finlay, Mia and Zara

Contents

Acknowledgments

Few books open with a word of thanks for the men and women of Scotland's police service but it seems fitting to do just that. If the chapters which follow do nothing else, they serve to illustrate the challenges faced by those tasked with keeping us, our money and our possessions safe and secure in the face of quite incredible challenges. The same applies to those working in the security industry who put their own safety on the line every day they get up and go to work.

No book I have worked on has been a solo effort and this project was no different. From those who lent me their time to speak on the record and share their expertise and memories – Jean Pandelus and Douglas Campbell – to the many who did likewise in an 'off-the-record' manner, the input was valuable. So too was the input from all at Birlinn, from the earliest stage of the project through to the finished article, and Colin Macleod with his continued keen eye and now legendary enthusiasm.

I must also thank the many journalists whose attention to detail, from the 18th century through to the modern day, has helped to preserve intricate detail from which many lessons have been and will continue to be learned.

Most importantly of all, my heartfelt appreciation goes to the most treasured people in my life and the source of eternal inspiration and support – Coral, Finlay, Mia and Zara.

Introduction

Heist – a single word but one which conjures up images of well-planned and well-oiled criminal machines, carrying out daring raids in an *Ocean's Eleven* style with precision and a degree of charm. Step away from the cinematic portrayals and the glamorous image of the dashing raider and what you find instead is, in fact, a harsh reality that is darker and far grimmer.

Lives have been lost and survivors scarred physically and mentally by those who have made it their mission to get their hands on other people's money and valuables by any means.

From the outset, the intention of *Heist* was never to glamorise or sensationalise the crimes detailed in the chapters which follow. Instead, the motivation was to catalogue some of the most notable episodes in Scotland's criminal history and to revisit incidents which, for very different reasons, made a lasting impact on those who found themselves caught up in them.

The sums involved run into tens of millions of pounds but monetary value is a poor barometer in this particular sphere. In every case, there is a human cost which is far more difficult to quantify but far greater than any financial loss.

The breadth of the enterprises covered in the pages of this book paints a picture of the lengths some will go to simply to profit. From murderous attacks to subtle sleight of hand and forgery, there is no textbook heist.

The research process threw up some common threads and familiar patterns, particularly the constant threat of armed robberies. That is something which has existed for centuries and looks set to continue to be a scourge of society for as long as weapons exist. Just as significantly, it also demonstrated the probability of the villains being caught – which is high. There is a misconception that those with, for want of a better word, the courage to carry out high-profile heists can get rich quick if they get the detail right. The truth is that very few have succeeded in escaping detection. Sometimes it is instant while on other occasions it may take weeks, months or years – but, eventually, past actions have had a habit of catching up with the culprits. If there is a crumb of comfort for the victims of these crimes, surely that is it.

What is clear is that there is no such thing as the perfect crime. Even in those rare cases which remain unsolved and where the proceeds have not been traced, mistakes were always made which gave police impetus for their investigation and positive lines to follow. The fear of a knock on the door must always be there for those who, so far, have evaded capture.

History shows that robbery is not a modern phenomenon, as some cases within *Heist* demonstrate, but, as time moves on, so does technology. The underworld is being forced to try to keep pace with those advances but there is little doubt that life on the wrong side of the fence is being made tougher all the time. From that, we can all take reassurance. But, as long as there is greed, there will always be temptation. Scotland will remain a target but it will not be just among the 'local' criminal fraternity. From European gangs staging million-pound jewel snatches to cross-border raiders travelling from England, *Heist* explores a number of incidents in which the finger of suspicion points beyond the home borders.

It also delves into the world of art and antiquities – a black market whose worth, globally, is close to that of illegal narcotics – as well as into high-tech raids of stolen computer equipment with a value that would have been unimaginable to those guilty of the far earlier crimes of cash thefts and the 'traditional' bank robbery.

Everything from escapes by bicycle, descents through ceilings and the use of JCB diggers to curious cases of the theft of much vaunted rhinoceros heads and priceless paintings by the masters are covered in the following pages. Which takes it back to where we started and cinema script comparisons. These real-life heists are not as you see them in the movies. All too often, the truth is more far-fetched than fiction.

1

Hitting the Heights

Brutal. Meticulous. Terrifying. Efficient. All four of those words applied in equal measure when a violent gang smashed its way into a Scottish security depot in 1998 to carry out what, to this day, remains one of Britain's biggest unsolved robberies. It was not just the £1.3-million cash haul or the military-style precision that set the well-drilled villains apart from their criminal peers – their modus operandi also proved unique. After all, why use a door when there is a perfectly suitable roof to provide a point of entry with that all-important element of surprise?

When the masked raiders brandishing shotguns crashed through the ceiling of the Securitas base in Aberdeen on a dark December evening, it marked the start of a horrific ordeal for the shell-shocked staff who had their lives threatened during the course of what was Scotland's biggest-ever armed robbery. But that night's events also marked the end of a long and methodical planning process for a group who succeeded in pulling off what most would have deemed impossible. Even the police officers investigating the crime were left aghast at the audacity of the slick crew, describing their actions as 'very quick, very efficient and very well planned'.

To escape with more than £1 million in cash from the heart of a busy commercial zone displayed a sense of arrogance and aggressive determination seldom seen before or since in Scotland, leaving detectives frustrated and the victims traumatised. A £250,000 reward still sits unclaimed and the police file remains open in the hope that, one day, those responsible will be brought to justice. With every passing year, that looks more and more forlorn, with any thought of recovering the seven-figure sum long since passed for the authorities who were left chasing shadows in the hunt for the perpetrators of what appears to have been the perfect heist.

The target for one of the most remarkable robberies ever carried out on Scottish soil sat in wholly unremarkable surroundings. As Europe's oil capital, Aberdeen has benefited from billions of pounds of wealth pouring into the region – but the industrial zones servicing the burgeoning energy industry are far from glamorous.

Altens, home to Securitas at the time of the raid, is one of those districts which sprung up to cater for the booming demand for business space. Not surprisingly, the oil industry grew up around Aberdeen's gritty docklands but, as the sector flourished, its reach spread wider. First came development in nearby Torry, a community which had thrived on the back of the fishing industry, and then came rapid expansion in the Tullos area to the south of the city centre. Beyond Tullos and its now ageing buildings lies Altens, a maze of industrial and office buildings constructed during the 1980s and 90s to keep up with demand. Situated on the southern edge of Aberdeen, transport links to Dundee and the Central Belt, via the A90 dual carriageway, are perfect. As the 1998 raid demonstrated, the easy exit routes were not only a boon for the commuters keen to flit south at the close of business but also for those with more sinister reasons for making a swift exit.

With oil giants such as Shell sitting side by side with one-man-band engineering outfits, busy scrapyards and office blocks, the Tullos and Altens industrial estates are a hive of activity morning, noon and night. Until December 1998, Securitas had been just another tenant on the area's Souterhead Road. And then everything changed.

Renamed to carry the Loomis brand in 2007, Securitas was the major player in the cash-in-transit (CIT) industry. At depots throughout Britain, it would take delivery of millions of pounds in cash deposits each day from businesses and financial institutions, with the firm a dominant force throughout the

1990s and beyond. At one stage Securitas was said to be handling around 40 per cent of all the money being transported on a daily basis in Britain.

Once the cash had been collected or delivered from a central distribution point, a fleet of armoured security vans could be fed to enable deliveries to bank branches and cashpoints in each region. The network was vital to keeping cash flowing, with speed of the essence. The vans, an obvious target for underworld gangs, were incredibly well protected. Sophisticated tracking devices ensured their every movement was monitored and any variation on the well-planned routes and daily schedules would immediately be flagged up to the highly trained command teams. The cash boxes used to carry money by foot from the vehicles to their eventual destination during the various stops on each round were fitted with ink canisters designed to render the currency worthless if tampered with by would-be thieves, making smash-and-grab attempts pointless. The only point at which cash was freely handled was in the sanctuary of the well-guarded depots, the hubs at the centre of the Securitas empire.

The sheer number of vehicle movements and quantities of notes being ferried from point to point meant it was impossible to keep a running total of how much was being held at any one point and, when the company did fall victim to high-profile robberies, it often took an unexpectedly long period of time to put a value to the missing money.

The most high-profile of all was at the Securitas depot at Tonbridge in Kent early in 2006 – when £53 million was netted in the largest heist Britain has ever seen. It was not until a full internal audit had been carried out that the staggering total could be confirmed. That headline-grabbing incident sent shockwaves around the world and sparked one of the biggest manhunts Britain has ever seen, with investigations stretching as far as Morocco as suspects were trailed across the globe.

The Tonbridge raid had an unbelievable air surrounding it but it was very real. It also sparked vivid memories for the Securitas staff who had been caught up in the Scottish forerunner eight years earlier. The Aberdeen robbery involved a far smaller haul but there were similarities both in the planning and the timing. In England, the cash was snatched in February, when it is thought robbers were confident of a sizeable return for their day's work thanks to an influx of money generated by retailers during the post-Christmas sales.

In the Scottish equivalent, the thieves also chose the festive period, opting for a pre-Christmas date when the tills were ringing and notes were flowing back and forth between shops and the depot. With every detail seemingly covered during the planning stages, it is inconceivable to think the date was not a matter for significant deliberation.

Location too must have been a factor. Could it have been a local gang or had the potential rewards from the oil-rich city in the north-east of Scotland reached a wider audience? In many ways Aberdeen has hidden its light under a bushel since the oil boom. With oil comes money and the soaring success of the energy industry has led to decade after decade of rising wages and a corresponding strengthening of the entire local economy. Retail has benefited, with Aberdeen ranking among the leading shopping destinations in Britain according to recent research findings and national chains stating that their stores in the city outperform most areas outside of London. Consequently, cash movements are large and frequent as the flood of spending is catered for.

The Aberdeen base of Securitas operated just like every other, with security its top priority. Although set in what appeared from the outside to be an ostensibly standard industrial unit on a run-of-the-mill road within the Altens business district, it was kitted out with a string of defences against unwanted attention.

On the exterior, the building, with its standard-issue yellow brick facade and red PVC cladding, was protected by external bollards and a specially reinforced door to prevent entry being gained by ram-raiding. There was a conscious effort to make sure physical barriers were in place to act as a deterrent against brute-force methods with only subtle signage, a proliferation of security cameras and purposeful metal bars on the inside of the frosted windows hinting at the nature of the unit's high-value contents. Unfortunately for Securitas, those precautions did not extend beyond ground level.

Inside, the usual array of CCTV technology was complemented by a similarly comprehensive selection of alarms. Set up to be triggered by everything from motion to body heat, they ensured that anyone who did find a way in would quickly be detected. With the alarms feeding directly to Grampian Police headquarters in the nearby city centre, a swift response was guaranteed in the event of an SOS being raised. Staff also had the added safety net of the building's manual panic alarms, again offering a direct line to police HQ.

Whilst managers and the company's army of security specialists were comfortable with the efforts they had taken to guard their stock of sterling, they had not bargained on the lengths some are prepared to go to in order to get rich quick – nor had they taken into account the ingenuity of the criminal fraternity.

There is only conjecture as to when the groundwork was done. Police believe the raid was months in the planning but know for certain that the gang responsible was active in the Aberdeen area for at least two weeks prior to the December 3 robbery. They could be sure of that because the getaway cars were stolen in the city in the fortnight leading up to the major incident as the foundations for the well-orchestrated mission were laid.

Nobody thought there was a bigger picture being painted when two vehicles vanished from separate locations in the Aberdeen area. Car theft was not a major problem in the north-east in the 1990s but occasional incidents ensured suspicion was not aroused by what appeared to be random and unconnected offences. But in fact there was nothing random about the two incidents inked in the Grampian Police crime log for November 1998. The vehicles stolen were hand-picked by a group who knew exactly what they were looking for and had combed the streets in search of the models on their wish list.

The first was a Vauxhall Senator saloon car, a model which

had become the darling of police forces up and down the country thanks to its hearty performance. The Senator became a familiar sight decked out in emergency livery, particularly on motorway patrols where it could eat up the miles and keep pace with even the most powerful of supercars with a maximum speed in the region of 150 mph at the top end of the range. In its most modern guise, it was active between 1987 and 1993, before being superseded in the Vauxhall line-up. Many officers mourned the loss of a faithful servant, viewed as the perfect police vehicle. Conversely, the big beast of a Vauxhall also made the ideal getaway car.

But one vehicle was never going to be enough for the size-able gang – they needed a second, more practical addition to their fleet to take care of personnel transportation as well as for coping with the sheer volume of notes they aimed to secure during their smash and grab. For that, they had opted for a Bedford Midi, a nondescript but reliable panel van that would not draw attention as it threaded its way through commuter traffic en route to its destination. Both of the stolen vehicles were white – a factor just as crucial to the thieves as getting the right make and model.

The clear train of thought among those who investigated the robbery is that several visits would have been paid to the site for reconnaissance purposes, with every inch of the surround-ing area plotted and every mile of the escape route trialled in advance. There was far too much at stake to risk mistakes and the work done in the months leading up to the raid would have been seen as vital as the actions on the night itself.

The beauty of the Aberdeen depot's location was not that it was isolated, as might be expected to be the preferred option. Instead, it was in the middle of a busy industrial estate, populated by multinational oil and gas companies receiving multiple deliveries by HGV each day and smaller enterprises attracting a steady stream of visitors and vehicle move-ments. That meant the gang could ghost around the area in the planning stages without any fear of being apprehended. Even today, with the experience of 1998, it is possible to sit undisturbed outside the unit, take notes and wander unhindered around the area. There is no perimeter fence, just an open car park and grassed areas. The process of formulating the heist plan would have been a comfortable one for a group clearly studious in its approach.

With the blueprint drawn up and the theory in place, the first stage of putting the plan into practice was sourcing the two getaway vehicles. What happened to those cars in the two-week period between their theft in Aberdeen and their reappearance at the depot remains a mystery. Storing those cars in the open air would have been a huge gamble – all it would have taken would have been for an eagle-eyed police officer to spot the rogue vehicles after they had been reported stolen and a chain of events would have been triggered that would have jeopardised the whole operation. On that basis, it is fair to assume the perpetrators had access to a garage or storage facility for that period. Where that was located is one of the key missing pieces in the police jigsaw.

Again the issue boiled down to a crucial factor – was this a local gang the authorities were seeking? If it was, then storing two stolen vehicles may not have been an issue. Access to garage premises, whether residential or industrial, would have been relatively straightforward and neither the car nor the van was likely to draw any undue attention. However, had these been visiting criminals it would have been a different story altogether. They would have had to source storage, presumably renting space undercover unless brave enough to leave two stolen vehicles parked in public and potentially open to recovery. They needed to be sure they would be available and would not have been keen to drive them in the period between their theft and the robbery itself.

Being caught behind the wheel of those two vehicles was not the only risk the robbers had to run in the build-up to their moment of reckoning. Just days before they carried out the crime, it is thought at least one member of the gang was sent to the Securitas warehouse to remove a roof panel which would help them gain entry. Not surprisingly for a building of its ilk, an alarm was triggered during that aerial activity – but inspections on the back of the alert failed to spot anything untoward, with the patrol apparently not stretching as far as the roof, and it was put down as a false alarm. It is possible the alarm being set off during that stage of the process was part of the plan, offering the chance to test police response times and providing a means to set an accurate timetable for the main event.

Timing was central to the ruthlessly efficient plan as it swung into operation on Thursday, 3 December 1998. Four of the six-strong group had positioned themselves on the roof of the building in the early evening, just as most of the workers in the surrounding buildings were preparing to head home after a day's work. Dressed all in black and wearing balaclavas, they were described as an SAS-style gang and, under the cover of darkness, succeeded in reaching their entry point without being spotted.

They lay in wait until a security van arrived to make a delivery. As the vehicle slipped quietly in through the electronic roller doors, the raiders made their move. When guards at ground level began to remove cash in heavyweight sacks from the newly arrived van, the assailants abseiled 12 feet down ropes from the gap in the ceiling they had broken through – a horrifying moment for the Securitas employees, who suddenly faced a quartet of shotgun-toting attackers. The five security personnel at work inside the building were threatened by the gunmen and could only look on in terror at what had begun as an ordinary night at work now descended into a scene resembling something from a Hollywood movie – a real-life *Ocean's Eleven* but without the sugar coating.

At the same time as the assailants rounded up the guards, all the time threatening to open fire, the Vauxhall Senator and Bedford van stolen to order by the group arrived at the scene. Driven by the remaining two members of the team, the vehicles were quickly ushered through the entrance door – with employees under duress to smooth their passage. With the getaway vehicles safely inside and away from prying eyes on the outside, the boot of the Senator and rear doors of the van were popped open and the loading process began. The money bags were so large and heavy, stuffed full of carefully bundled notes, they could not be lifted by the raiders. Instead, it took them all their strength to drag the sacks to the rear of the vehicles and heave them inside. All in all, they had loaded £1.3 million in a matter of minutes, not pausing or deviating from the script.

The entire episode inside the faceless industrial unit lasted no more than quarter of an hour from the moment the masked robbers made their shock entrance through the roof to their exit by car and van, with the roller door lifted to enable them to drive unchallenged from the building and into the crisp winter's night.

A brave guard had managed to activate a panic alarm during his ordeal, despite the shotgun deterrent, but, by the time police arrived at the scene, it was too late. Units had been scrambled from a series of surrounding police stations as well as from the Queen Street HQ, racing to the south of the city with sirens blaring and lights piercing the dark sky. But the well-drilled gang had already made their escape – and pointedly had chosen to do so whilst additional bags of cash remained in the depot and were theirs for the taking. They had refused to let the lure of additional gain cloud their judgement and stuck rigidly to what appears to have been a predetermined schedule for the length of time they could afford to spend at the scene. It was another demonstration of the cold and calculating nature of the men responsible. It was a disciplined and professional operation.

Throughout the robbery they were meticulous in their efforts to preserve their anonymity. Faces were never exposed and only one man spoke – the cool and composed individual victims classed as the gang leader. He barked his instructions in a distinctive Cockney accent, adding to the already established theory that the perpetrators were an experienced organised crime gang from south of the border. Such was the slick execution of the master plan, detectives were convinced they were not dealing with first-time offenders or opportunistic locals.

For the whole duration of the drama, there was an eerie sense of calm surrounding proceedings. Aside from the ringleader's assertive instructions, it was conducted in silence with clockwork precision. Workers at neighbouring premises were oblivious to the shocking scene unfolding in the adjoining building. The Securitas depot sat on the edge of a horseshoe of small units, sheltered by a band of trees and shrubbery adjacent to its exterior wall but, in such confined surroundings, it is astonishing that the activity on the early evening in question did not attract attention.

Just as the robbery had been carefully plotted, the getaway was far from an afterthought. It was then that the choice of vehicles – and in particular the choice of white for both the car and van – came into their own as the drivers produced flashing blue lights to mount on the dashboards. To members of the public both vehicles had the appearance of unmarked police vehicles and drivers moved aside to allow them easy passage through the traffic which so often clogs up the busy industrial parks of Aberdeen.

From the inner-city surroundings of Souterhead Road, the two-car pack cut through the suburban commuter village of Cove as the scenery quickly flicked from town to country. Cove, perched on clifftops hugging the east shore to the south of the city, provides a gateway to a network of coastal roads and lanes servicing the agricultural land in the area. The robbers used that to their advantage as they disappeared into the night, travelling at speed along a route they must surely have rehearsed time after time as they perfected the dash for freedom.

With stone dykes and ditches lining the rutted surfaces, the cross-country sprint was not one for the faint-hearted and the fact it was conducted in pitch dark adds even more weight to the assumption that the drivers chosen for the role had experience and ability behind the wheel.

Within 25 minutes of the alarm being raised at the depot, Grampian Police had established a series of roadblocks on all key routes leading to and from Aberdeen in an effort to snare the gang. But the raiders were one step ahead throughout the night in question and ensured they used little-known minor roads to speed them away from the scene of the crime, never venturing close to the main arteries. The path took them at breakneck speed through the tiny fishing village of Findon and into Portlethen, another commuter outpost, for the next stage of their bid to evade the authorities during a rapid four-mile dart away from Altens. Had it not been for a report of a Vauxhall Senator being driven erratically in the town by a concerned member of the public, the route would have been protected for even longer.

There was, as with all heists of this magnitude, an element of luck involved. For all the planning and plotting that had been carried out, the getaway path was one which was fraught with danger. As it was single-track for stages of the road, the raiders would have been hoping for a clear run. This was rural Aberdeenshire after all – one tractor blocking the road, one herd of cattle being moved from field to field and the whole operation could have been thrown into jeopardy. As they shuttled past the neat bungalows lining the road in Findon, they knew the worst was over and the home stretch was in sight.

In addition to being contacted about the Senator's haste, witnesses also came forward to tell police that at least one passenger from the two vehicles had been seen being dropped off in the car park of the Asda superstore in Portlethen. The presumption is the next in the chain of getaway vehicles was parked outside the store, inconspicuous among row upon row of cars visiting the busy supermarket for more legitimate purposes.

The final resting place for the Senator and the Bedford van was on waste ground behind Portlethen Parish Church, perched on a hillside and surrounded by grassland. The church offers a good vantage point over the neighbouring residential and commercial areas, suggesting it was a carefully selected location rather than a hastily chosen dumping ground. In the shadow of the imposing granite kirk, the remaining members of the gang unloaded the vehicles and torched them in an effort to destroy any forensic evidence before vanishing – complete with £1.3 million of Securitas' funds. It was only when a local resident spotted flames licking into the sky from the rear of the building and contacted the fire service that police were able to piece together the movements of the group they had been trying in vain to trace.

Within hours of the robbery, Grampian's finest had assembled a team of 40 officers to investigate the heist. There was a tremendous public response to the initial appeal for information, with detectives and uniformed colleagues interviewing hundreds of witnesses. They spent time visiting businesses throughout Altens and left no stone unturned in their quest for vital clues. Staff at the cash depot were also quizzed at length, with officers duty bound to explore the possibility that the raiders may have had help from the inside. That was not a theory that was ever publicly discussed or given credence by the investigating team.

A painstaking forensic examination of the Securitas premises and the nearby ground was conducted as experts from across the force's various disciplines joined together for one of the most significant investigations in the history of law enforcement in the north-east.

Securitas also redoubled its attention to its Altens branch in the aftermath of the raid, looking again at the measures in place to preserve the integrity of the building. It was the first time the firm had suffered a robbery at any of its Scottish bases and the repercussions reverberated throughout the company. The five staff members targeted by the raiders all underwent counselling as they came to terms with the impact of an armed robbery.

Incredibly the loss of £1.3 million did not impact on cash flow in the city, with Securitas quickly able to bridge the gap in supply to prevent disruption. Robbery or no robbery, the show must go on. As the cash-handling company attempted to return to normality, police set about gathering CCTV footage from neighbouring properties to join the film taken within the depot on the night of the raid. Detectives took the decision to release the video for public consumption, with images showing the guards being held at gunpoint, and this stirred another wave of calls to the incident desk.

The raid, which had already been the subject of intense press coverage throughout December 1998, benefited from national exposure as a reconstruction on the BBC's *Crimewatch* programme was played out late in January 1999. Again the attention prompted snippets of additional information from viewers but not the breakthrough the investigation team was hoping for.

As has so often been the case, landing a prime spot on *Crimewatch* was a major strike for the investigating team. Since the first show was broadcast in 1984, it has been a vital tool for officers keen to reach out beyond the confines of their own force area. The Securitas robbery had been big news in the north-east and relatively so in Scotland as a whole, but tapping into the English audience was seen as key. There was never any assumption that the criminal network was small and spreading the reach of the appeal for information was an important part of the strategy.

The lack of concrete leads was all the more frustrating given the huge rewards on offer for positive information. Within a week of the crime, Securitas had put the lure of £150,000 on the table. That figure later rose to £250,000 but, so far, the company has not had to dig out its chequebook to pay the bounty. The trail had gone cold, even if the evidence pointed towards one of England's crime gangs.

Criminologists believe as few as three major criminal enterprises were responsible for the bulk of major heists across Britain during the late 1990s and early part of the new millennium. Their targets were said to stretch well beyond British shores, with intelligence suggesting even Germany's gold reserves were not safe from the reach of UK thieves as they plotted even more daring and ambitious missions from safe houses on British shores.

Grampian Police were keen to explore links between their own investigation and other work being undertaken by forces elsewhere in the country. Following the £53-million episode at Tonbridge in 2006, officers from Aberdeen co-operated with Kent counterparts to compare notes on the record-breaking heist and the smaller but similar incident in Scotland. Just as in the Scottish raid, the thieves had used getaway cars designed to appear like unmarked police vehicles – one of a number of similarities. Unlike the Scottish robbery, detectives recovered large quantities of cash during the course of their lengthy investigations in England and made a series of arrests both in Britain and abroad. Six men were eventually found guilty at trial of playing a part in the Kent heist, with other suspects either cleared of the charges or still at large.

Those convictions took place a decade after the Aberdeen raid and Grampian Police detectives returned to the limelight in 2008 to issue a fresh appeal for help in cracking their own case. The file remains open although the hopes of ever gaining a conclusion by bringing suspects to court remain a fading dream for those who were left stumped by a carefully choreographed and perfectly executed heist.

2

The Ibrox Open Goal

It was described at the time as Scotland's biggest bank robbery and one of the best planned the country had ever seen. It also had as one of its main suspects a man billed as the Monocled Major and one of Glasgow's most recognisable districts as its backdrop – in short, the Ibrox heist of 1955 had all the ingredients to make it a headline writer's dream.

It is no surprise that the crime did indeed hog the front pages, with news of the audacious and meticulously executed raid spreading far and wide within hours. In return, police were fed with leads from as far afield as London as one of the biggest investigations Scotland has ever seen took officers from their traditional inner city beat into the wilds of rural Perthshire and the unfamiliar stomping grounds of England's counties.

At the centre of the furore was a missing £44,000 haul – the equivalent of close to £1 million in 2014 terms. The money was liberated from the British Linen Bank when a cash van was hijacked as it made its daily delivery rounds. The team responsible for the broad-daylight raid had been as cold as it had been calculating, willing to use violent force to carry through with its carefully plotted blueprint.

Just how well considered the episode had been began to crystallise as the investigation matured. Detectives at the heart of the case revealed they suspected it may have been five years in the planning, a measure of the attention to detail which had been a hallmark of the gang.

After apparently careful deliberation, they struck on 19 July

1955. It was the Tuesday of Glasgow's Fair Holiday week, with the city quieter than usual and the traffic calmer than might otherwise have been expected. It was perfect for a quick and unhindered getaway.

The chosen location was Ibrox, more specifically Paisley Road West and the bustling district's branch of the British Linen Bank. Just after 9.30 a.m., a red van drew up outside the bank with a crew of three assigned to make cash deliveries across the city that day. They were early in their shift, as they snaked their way across the city, and had no reason to suspect it would be anything other than an ordinary day's work.

The driver and one of the messengers left the van to carry money bags to the bank and, as they did, the robbers struck. Knocking the remaining crew member unconscious in the back of the van, they sped off through the traffic and away from the scene . . . with money spilling out of the back as they did so.

In today's ultra-cautious, security-conscious era, there is a sense of incredulity at one of the crucial facets of the heist – the key to the van, despite its high-value cargo, had been left in the ignition. This was a robbery made easy.

The takeaway, in many respects, was simple. The getaway, as with so many crimes of a similar nature, was a more testing proposition.

The van was soon discovered abandoned in the driveway of an unoccupied villa at 7 Dumbreck Road. The terrified crew member was found trussed up in the van, left helpless, and the bulk of contents had gone. The raiders had driven less than a mile from the scene of the crime before apparently switching vehicles and spiriting the proceeds away from the city. They left behind bags of coins, presumably deemed too bulky to transport easily.

Not surprisingly, the raid made big headlines in the days that followed. *The Glasgow Herald*, reporting on the incident for the first time, described it as one of 'the best-planned robberies' Scotland had ever seen. *The Bulletin* described it as 'Scotland's biggest bank robbery' and, arguably, that claim still holds true. The paper noted that the robbers had 'an obvious knowledge of the distributive organisation' involved in sending money from the British Linen Bank head office to the network of branches in Glasgow. The Ibrox outlet was the second stop of the day. Apart from the money that had been delivered at the van's initial stop in Eglinton and the cash that had already been taken into the Ibrox branch just before the team struck, the van was practically fully laden.

The British Linen Bank has long since disappeared from the consciousness of consumers, but at the time of the robbery it was still a major player on the Scottish financial scene. Founded in the 1700s in Edinburgh, as the name suggests, it had its roots in the linen industry but quickly established a foothold in the banking sector. The network of branches quickly expanded, with more than 100 across the country by the turn of the 20th century. Bought by Barclays in 1919, by the Second World War, there were 170 branches in Scotland and it continued to operate successfully until it was sold to Bank of Scotland. The name eventually disappeared from branches, but until 1999 it was still used as the umbrella for the merchant arm of Bank of Scotland. However, in the 1950s its branches were significant targets as far as members of Scotland's criminal underbelly were concerned.

Details of the raid quickly began to filter into the public domain, with police revealing that four men had surrounded the van after it had parked outside the Ibrox branch. With the driver and his assistant inside making a cash drop, the watching rogues sprang into action in a carefully choreographed routine. Two jumped into the cab while the other pair rushed into the rear of the van to disable the remaining employee – messenger Lindsay Currie. The assailants drove off along Gower Street, into Sherbrooke Avenue and on towards Pollokshields. Currie's shouts for help were heard by his colleagues, who emerged from the bank to see the van being taken. Quick-thinking driver Gilbert Tait, just 24 at the time, commandeered a passing lorry and gave chase – but he was unable to keep pace with the bank van. Incredibly, just a day later, Tait was back on his rounds and delivering to the same branch. For his injured colleague Currie, 10 days of bed rest was the doctor's order.

Although the chase proved fruitless, it did not take long for the stolen bank van to be located. It was found just 15 minutes at the empty house on Dumbreck Road when a woman near the scene heard Currie's cries and went to his aid. The elderly eyewitness, Elizabeth Duncan, told reporters, 'A van was standing with its doors open – I could just see a man's legs hunched up. He was lying across the back of the van.'

Trees and shrubbery provided natural screening around the property, which had been unoccupied since the war years when it was utilised by the army, making it the perfect location for switching vehicles – which was the theory police worked on too after a report from the neighbourhood that four men were seen at the same house, arriving in a black saloon car. The description of an Austin A40 was circulated after a worker at the nearby Bellahouston bowling green had recalled details of the car seen at the house. That was part of a huge police operation, with patrol cars from across Glasgow converging on the area. They attempted to lock down the area and began a systematic search but to no avail.

Meanwhile, Currie was taken to the Victoria Infirmary suffering from a head injury and shock. He was allowed to return home after treatment. The assailants had at least removed the gag from Currie's mouth before they left him and made their getaway, a small concession after their ruthless ambush but one which enabled the van to be located far more quickly than it otherwise might have been. It was the first sign of cracks in the plan.

Although it was believed the gang had made their exit by car, police also investigated claims by a local resident that four men, walking in pairs, had been seen on foot in Bellahouston Park at around the same time. They were last seen running off in the direction of Paisley Road West, with one said to have a large bruise on the side of his face. They were all pieces of the jigsaw that was being slotted together. Another line of enquiry related to a theft reported soon after the bank van had been targeted although, this time, it was a more modest £55 which had been stolen, snatched from an open safe at a petrol station on the Glasgow to Kilmarnock road. Three or four men in a grey Wolseley, one of whom was said to have had up to £200 in banknotes in his hand, pulled up at the Turf Petrol Station, near Loganswell, within hours of the Ibrox incident. As they filled up with fuel, one was said to have slipped inside and taken the money from the open safe.

That was one of a string of reports that stemmed from the publicity surrounding the case. On the evening of the robbery, another petrol station attendant had his suspicions aroused when two men in a 1931 Vauxhall pulled up at his forecourt in Bridgeton and acted oddly and irritably, paying with a British Linen Bank £1 note and wearing sunglasses despite the fact it was nearly 9 p.m. That was another lead for the stretched police team to follow up but far from the last.

A length of rope left behind in the van, used to tie up Currie, was another positive line of enquiry. It was described as 'relatively new' and officers were tasked with taking samples around various stores in Glasgow to try and track down its roots. It was a thankless task but a sign of the determination within the investigating team to leave no stone unturned.

Detectives said hundreds of leads had been logged within the first two days of the investigation but expressed frustration that sources in the Glasgow underworld scene were not talking. That silence was possibly a case of honour among thieves but consideration was also given to the possibility that there was genuinely no local knowledge of the bank job which had become the talk of the steamie. Could it be that a London gang was behind the crime? Officers certainly thought it was a possibility and roads between Scotland and England were subjected to intense police activity as vehicles were stopped and searched.

Again, there was an element of bad fortune surrounding that task and the search parameters were not aided by the circumstances of the heist. It transpired that the majority of the notes – all but around £1,000 – were in untraceable denominations

of 10s, £1 or £5. Only the serial numbers of larger notes had
been logged by the bank. It was feasible, given the extent of
the planning which appeared to have gone into the exercise,
that those responsible were well aware that their haul would be
'clean' and able to be pushed into circulation without arousing
suspicion.

It was Glasgow's head of CID, Chief Detective Superintendent Gilbert McIlwrick, who headed the investigation
with Chief Detective Inspector Robert Kerr and Chief
Detective Inspector James McAulay leading on the ground.
Their investigations took them across Britain as they attempted
to track down witnesses and suspects, with around 300 people
interviewed as part of the probe. Resources were poured into
the case as police, no doubt under pressure from out-of-pocket
bank chiefs, pushed for a positive result. They were dealing
with a well-drilled team of crooks but, fortunately for detectives, this was not a flawless crime. The crew responsible for
the robbery were undone by a silly mistake. When they fled
Dumbreck Road, abandoning the bank van, they left behind
the uniforms they had adopted to help them avoid drawing
attention to themselves as they lay in wait at Ibrox.

Those brown dustcoats appeared relatively indistinguishable
but police latched on to laundry markings and initials on the
labels. For the first time ever, Scottish officers also harnessed
the power of the modern media by turning to television for
help – appearing on the small screen with the dustcoats in
a plea for help in tracing their origins. That appeal went far
and wide hitting the target in London, of all places, when an
AA patrolman by the name of Frank Buckingham recognised
the initials as his own and also told police that he had lent
the dustcoats to a man in London, thus providing a name for
police to pursue.

Slowly, the case began to slot together. A week after the robbery, police in Perth recovered a black Rover 60 which they
believed had been used in the robbery. It had been left in a
car park in the town on 20 July, the night after the cash was
snatched, and never reclaimed. Examinations revealed it was

bearing false registration plates and tax disc, having been stolen in London two months earlier. Fingerprints were discovered in the abandoned car and yet another clue was added to the bulging case files.

At the same time, detectives travelled from Glasgow to London to liaise with Scotland Yard colleagues over the information provided about the dustcoats. Initially it was reported it had been stolen from the AA patrolman's car, although it was later suggested he had lent it to one of the men who soon became one of a number accused of being involved in the theft. It was a significant turning point in the probe.

The first arrest in the case took place in September 1955 – not in Glasgow but in Dublin. Couples dancing to soft music in the Dun Laoghaire Hotel in the Irish capital watched in shock as a fellow guest was led, handcuffed to a detective, from the building. That man was John Charles Lappen. Australian-born but a resident of England for many years, he had been staying at the hotel with his wife, who was also spoken to by police, and their room was searched. The net was closing on the Ibrox gang, with the police stretching far beyond their usual confines to bring the investigation to a conclusion.

Days prior to that, as the investigation gathered pace, an application had been made in a Dublin court for the release of two men from Mountjoy Prison. One of them, Charles McGuinness, would later be sentenced for his part in the Glasgow robbery. The other, a Londoner, was never the subject of court proceedings.

In October, the operation moved to England as the intriguing character George Grey was apprehended in a hotel in Middlesbrough and arrested. He was the man believed to be the 'Monocled Major' who was said to be at the heart of the bank van robbery and who had in his possession a 'considerable' sum of money. He was the fifth man to be arrested by that stage, with two others in Dublin and two more in Glasgow.

By the time it came before the court, the case involved six men. John Charles Lappen, John Blundell, Charles McGuinness, Cornelius O'Donnell, John Bryden and

William White Thomson appeared on five charges relating to the £44,000 robbery. Accused of acting with George Grey during the alleged crime, they denied all the charges. A jury of eight men and seven women gathered on 9 January 1956 for the opening day of the trial, with Lord Patrick presiding at the High Court in Glasgow. It would prove to be an exhaustive process but one that captured the imagination of the Scottish public, who were following the daily updates with intensity.

Conspicuous by his absence was the Monocled Major. Chief Detective Inspector Robert Kerr said he was led to believe that there were provisions in the Criminal Justice Act which precluded the 'Major' from appearing in the dock. Close to £2,000 had been accounted for at the time of Grey's arrest, whilst Thomson had been found in possession of a holdall containing more than £3,000. Grey eventually appeared in court in September 1957. It had transpired that his absence from the original trial was due to a seven-year sentence he was already serving for safebreaking and robbery in Surrey. The Australian did, however, have to face the music north of the border too and was transferred from Wandsworth to Barlinnie in preparation for the court action.

John Lappen, aged 56, 45-year-old Englishman John Blundell and 43-year-old Scottish national Charles McGuinness were all found guilty of various charges relating to their involvement in the affair. Lappen was jailed for eight years and his two accomplices for six years each. Lappen died in 1960 after suffering a heart problem whilst in Saughton Prison. Charges against the others involved in the case were found not proven.

What the trial served to do was paint a picture of the build-up and aftermath of the Ibrox episode. Throughout the proceedings, the accused denied their involvement and explained their association was through involvement in horse-racing circles. That was also the assumption of many of those they encountered in the build-up, whilst ensconced in their temporary staging post in the wilds of Perthshire. The gang had chosen as their base the Rob Roy Roadhouse near Aberfoyle.

As the trial progressed, staff and guests were called to give evidence, recounting details of a gathering of the crew on the eve of the robbery. Nobody watching had any inkling of the plan being hatched but, with the benefit of hindsight, the telltale clues began to become evident. Staff suggested all of the accused, with the exception of Thomson, were staying at the isolated hotel. The 'Major', as Grey was referred to by the housekeeper, was said to have been an affable guest and the centre of attention. The party departed the day after the robbery, travelling in a Riley and a Rover. The Riley had been taken to a local garage during the group's stay for repairs to its clutch.

On the day the cash was snatched, a guest at the roadhouse reported seeing two men with bundles of money in one of the chalets at the complex. The Major was one; the other, she said, was John Blundell. She suggested there could have been as many as a dozen bundles of blue notes – the same colour used by the British Linen Bank. Other guests confirmed their belief in the horse-racing connection – conversations about race meetings in Scotland had been overheard, which tied in with the claims made by the accused men themselves.

In 1957, the roadhouse, which had been a feature in Perthshire since the 1930s, was renamed the Rob Roy Highland Motel but it did not stop newspapers using the occasion to bring up its intriguing past, flagging up the fact that a cache of cash could still be hidden somewhere in the vicinity. The greatest mystery of all was what had happened to the missing money. Around £6,000 was recovered during the investigation but that still left £38,000 unaccounted for. The search continued for years but enquiries drew a blank.

The assertion that the 'job' had been years in the making was repeated in court, with Lappen and McGuinness described as two of the principal 'brains' behind the operation. However, it was not only the suspects who found themselves in the dock – so too did the British Linen Bank, as its security procedures were put under very public scrutiny during the course of the trial.

On the opening day, evidence included startling revelations about the laxity in protocol. Driver Gilbert Tait admitted he had left the keys for the van in the ignition and Lindsay Currie, the messenger injured in the robbery, revealed the crew had been given no specific instructions designed to prevent the theft of their load. Tait said he agreed it may not have been wise to leave the keys but claimed it was 'done all the time' by the delivery drivers. Tait also confirmed he had been working for Patersons, the transport company contracted by the bank to carry out deliveries, for eight months. He was relatively new to the bank errands when the robbery occurred but admitted that the same route was followed each day and the same timetable followed. He would follow the routine four days per week, collecting a Patersons van from the firm's Ann Street depot and travelling to Queen Street, the HQ of the British Linen Bank, for it to be loaded by bank employees before the van departed for its deliveries.

On the day in question, it was stated that Tait and Charles McNeil, the other messenger, left Currie in the rear of the van as they made the drop at the Ibrox branch. Currie was busy arranging cash bags for the next delivery when the assailants sprang their unwanted surprise.

On the opening day of the trial, Tait identified the accused John Charles Lappen in court as the man he had seen dressed in a brown dustcoat and standing on the corner of Gower Street looking towards the van as the cash drop was made. Other witnesses told of a 'signal' used by the gang, with one appearing to slap a rolled-up piece of paper in the palm of his hand to instigate the well-choreographed operation.

There were lighter moments during a weighty trial with 10-year-old witness Jean Pandelus warming hearts with her testimony. Described in newspaper reports as having a 'shock of curly dark hair', the schoolgirl assured the court she knew it was wrong to 'tell fibs' and that she would tell the truth while on the witness stand. She confirmed that two men had come from a nearby telephone box and jumped in the van before it was driven away. More than half a century on, Jean Pandelus is now Jean Miller and can no longer be found in the Scottish climes of Glasgow but in the US state of Ohio. Decades have passed and a continent separates her from her homeland but the events of 1955 remain fresh in the mind of the courtroom star. Marriage took the Glaswegian across the Atlantic and to a new life but her links to the country of her birth remain strong and her interest in events on her old stomping ground are as keen as the day she departed in the 1960s.

Speaking from the comfort of her home in the American Midwest, Jean told me: 'I saw what I saw but it was my mum and aunt who really had a harder time of it – particularly my mum, who was an introvert really and didn't enjoy the attention the trial brought. It took a lot of courage for her to stand up in court and give evidence – something I know she wasn't comfortable with but she knew she had to go through with it.

'Even after the trial, it wasn't over. I remember my mum was stopped in the street by a man when she was walking along one day and asked if she had been involved in the court case. She was terrified he had something to do with those who had been convicted and tried to say she hadn't been. The man just said that he'd obviously been mistaken and that, in any case, he just wanted to tell the lady who had given evidence that one of the ringleaders had died in prison. She thanked him and went on her way – breathing a huge sigh of relief as she did. She was really shaken up by the whole thing.'

Just as her mother, May Pandelus, and aunt, Mina Slater, had to take to the witness stand, Jean also had her moment in the spotlight. She was called upon to recount the detail of her brush with the Monocled Major and his gang and impressed everyone with her efforts in court. Even now, she can recount the events of that day with clarity. She said: 'We were walking past a remodelling shop, full of wallpaper and paint and other decorating goods, when I saw the men standing close to the door. They were wearing brown overalls, presumably to try and look as though they were painters or plasterers.

'We saw the security guards come out of the van and go into

the bank – then all hell broke loose. The van took off down the road, nobody inside the bank had a clue though. My mum and aunt had seen everything and dashed inside to tell everyone what had happened. That's when the guards ran out and tried to give chase. I had seen it all but, at my age, I didn't really understand what was going on.

'Still, I was a witness like everyone else that day and the police treated me just the same despite my age. My mum really didn't want me to be involved and told them that but I still had to go along to a line-up to try to identify who I had seen. I was terrified. I didn't have good eyesight and couldn't recognise anyone – just as my mum had told them would be the case – but it didn't make any difference. I had to give evidence when the case made it to court and can still remember everything about that day, right down to being taken for lunch by a police-woman to try and make me feel more at ease.'

As it happened, the youngster was perfectly comfortable in the glare of a packed courtroom as one of Glasgow's biggest trials was played out. The media gallery was packed as report-ers attentively listened to every detail in the search of the next big headline – and that day they got their story.

Jean said: 'I ended up in all the newspapers. We lived at the Paisley Road Toll, right next to the Angel Building, and my mum would send me out to buy the *Daily Record* each morning. The day after I had given evidence, I picked up the paper in the shop to find a huge picture of myself staring back at me from the page. I was so embarrassed and it didn't just make the *Record* – it was in lots of different papers. My dad worked for MacBrayne's over on the west coast and he even found the picture and story in the *Oban Times*. When I went back to lessons at Rutland Crescent School, my teacher had me drawing pictures of my experience and telling my classmates all about it.

'I guess that was my 15 minutes of fame, with my mum and my aunt in the spotlight too. As I say, mum didn't enjoy that much at all – my aunt was far more gregarious though, so it didn't faze her at all to come out of court and be greeted with photographers trying to take our picture.'

Jean spent the rest of her childhood in Glasgow, moving to her adopted home in the US in 1966 after meeting her future husband, American Will Miller, and settling in the US where the couple brought up their children. Before moving overseas, there was still time for another brush with Glasgow's less desirable element. Jean said: 'When I was slightly older, I was out walking our dog when I stumbled across two men acting suspiciously around the basement of Thomson's piano store. I must have disturbed them trying to break in and they weren't best pleased – one of them karate chopped me, the other came at me with the box cutters he was carrying. Fortunately another man appeared on the scene and he must have known the other two and that stopped them in their tracks. I picked up the dog under my arm and made a run for it.'

Those two incidents have not spoilt the exiled Scot's memories of her childhood in Glasgow, with her contribution to the Ibrox heist trial locked away in her memory bank. It was the evidence of Jean Pandelus which took the story back to a key point, the moment at which the robbers made their escape before abandoning the vehicle and fleeing – leaving their dustcoats behind. The key point in the investigation was when the London-based AA man identified the man he had lent the recovered clothing to – and that person was John Blundell.

Blundell spoke in court of his surprise when police burst into the basement flat in Fulham in which he had been lying low. He admitted his part in the robbery to officers there and then, stressing he hadn't been involved in the assault on the messenger. With his admission, the case began to take shape although it was not until 1957 that it was finally concluded as Grey appeared at the High Court in Glasgow. The charges were familiar – he stood accused of assaulting a bank messenger and robbing him of £44,025. A plea of not guilty was entered by his solicitor, Harry McGoldrick.

Grey was charged with, while acting with John Charles Lappen, John Blundell and Charles McGuinness and other men on 19 July 1955, in a motor van in Paisley Road West, near Gower Street, assaulting Lindsay Cunningham Currie, of

Clarkston, who was then in charge of the van and its contents, and rendering him unconscious. It was further alleged that, during a journey by the van, between Paisley Road West and 7 Dumbreck Road, Glasgow, they bound the hands and legs of Currie with rope and his eyes and mouth with adhesive tape, to his severe injury, and robbed him of the motor van and £44,025 contained in six cases and a number of money bags. For the trial 145 crown witnesses were cited and 115 productions logged. At the end of it, Grey was sentenced to six years in prison for his role.

After serving time for his English indiscretions, he was eventually released in August 1964 and immediately set about suing the police for £750 in relation to clothes and property he said had been destroyed. The Monocled Major, it appeared, had no intention of going quietly.

3

A Sign of the Times

The Ibrox heist was like taking candy from a baby for the Monocled Major and his crew. With the van keys in the ignition and no way for the police to track it other than good old-fashioned line of sight, the banks were pretty much defenceless in the face of attacks on their delivery network in that era. Fast-forward half a century and today's cash-in-transit industry is far removed from those innocent times. Now, heavily armoured and reinforced vans are equipped with a bamboozling array of technology designed to deter thieves, whether opportunistic or highly organised.

From satellite tracking systems to CCTV cameras beaming live images of the delivery rounds back to base, every inch of the journey is covered. Even those who do manage to gain access are not on easy street, with systems for rendering stolen cash unusable in place and other gadgets straight from a James Bond movie being deployed. Lessons from the distant past have been learned and never again will criminals simply be able to drive away with a cash van and its contents – procedures and protocol will see to that. But, for all of the modern advances, the plague of cash van robberies has not been eradicated. If anything, the problem has grown at a rate which the police and long-suffering security firms have struggled to keep pace with.

Faced with increasingly stern defences, perpetrators are going to even more extreme lengths than ever before. From the subtle to the barbaric, such attacks have been alarmingly common in the recent criminal history of Scotland. On a bad week, experts report there can be as many as 15 assaults on cash-carrying security vans in Britain. It makes the cash-in-transit crew's job arguably one of the most dangerous in the country. That assertion was demonstrated most chillingly over the course of a three-month period in 2002 in the Lanarkshire town of Uddingston. Twice, crews making cash runs at the same Bank of Scotland branch were targeted in that short space of time, and on each occasion they were faced with a situation nightmares are made of. No bullets were fired, no baseball bats wielded, no knives brandished. Instead the raiders came armed with a weapon more unnerving than any of those, choosing petrol as the horrific means to an end.

In the first incident, on 25 September, a masked trio held staff at gunpoint as they threatened them with petrol. The fear of the raiders opening fire must have been very much secondary to the terror felt by those threatened with the prospect of being turned into human fireballs. It was a cold and calculating way of guaranteeing no resistance and enabled the thieves to make off with a considerable cash haul.

The Friday-night attack shattered the peace of Uddingston's Main Street, the traditional heart of the town and, until recent years, not a location mentioned frequently in connection with serious crime. That has now all changed, with a spate of incidents, but those involving petrol were by far the most sinister.

In the first case, the gang responsible made their escape in a car which had been stolen in Glasgow 10 days earlier. It was found abandoned shortly afterwards in nearby Bellshill Road. Investigating officers described it as a 'vicious and sustained attack' by a 'determined group of men' who displayed a 'blatant disregard' for the security guards' well-being.

In the second attack, on 13 December, one member of the Brinks Security staff was doused in fuel whilst one of the callous gang of thieves sparked a lighter and threatened to set him alight unless the security team parted with their cargo. Not surprisingly, they obeyed orders and, over the course of the two raids, made off with in the region of £350,000.

Police were confident that the same gang was responsible for both raids. Showing an arrogance to match their brutality, they returned to the scene of their earlier crime to carry out a second attack following the same script. One former detective claimed at the time that infamy as well as fortune may have been a driving force, stating: 'In prison and criminal circles, armed robbers are the aristocrats of the underworld. They get that misplaced respect, despite innocent people being terrorised and hurt during these robberies.

'There are easier ways for criminals to make money these days, through drugs and other gangland activities. It is, however, unusual for the same gang to use the same modus operandi and get away with it. It is possible they are looking for a bit of notoriety and are motivated, at least in part, by getting one over on the police.'

That expert opinion, formed with the benefit of dealing with rogues day in and day out, raises a spectre not confined to this particular chapter. Have some of Scotland's biggest heists been driven by a conviction that the crimes carry a perceived glamour that will attract media interest?

Glasgow's newspapers in particular have thrived on the apparently weekly updates and salacious tales from the city's underbelly. From the days of Arthur Thompson, arguably the first 'celebrity' gangster in the country, right through to the modern day and the many high-profile trials and murders in that particular scene, there have been miles and miles of copy generated. Editors would argue that public interest is at the root of the news agenda and that is ultimately and inevitably the case. Just as crime is fiction's greatest genre, the same too applies in the factual world of newspapers. And, if it helps sell papers, it will always find a space on the page.

Behind the headlines is a more human story, one rarely told. The Brinks employees were left traumatised by their experiences in what is normally a peaceful corner of the Central Belt. When they set out for work on those otherwise unremarkable days, there was no amount of training that could have prepared them for what lay ahead. The identical raids saw three balaclava-clad men pounce during evening collections from the Bank of Scotland branch. Their uniform of boiler suits became a familiar sight during a spate of raids during the period in question, with five in the Strathclyde area alone. The theory was that all were carried out by the same crew, one which was cash rich by the end of their spree having raked in hundreds of thousands of pounds along the way.

During the Uddingston petrol attacks, two members of the trio clutched guns as the third played menacingly with the naked flame from a lighter in front of the petrol-soaked guard. It would have taken little more than a spark flying in the wrong direction for what was apparently intended as a threat to become a matter of life and death.

Bags stuffed with money, fresh from the bank, were handed over by terrified colleagues in a desperate attempt to avoid their workmate being torched. With the bags surrendered, a waiting getaway car allowed the raiders to make a speedy exit. Meanwhile, their innocent victim was left to come to terms with what had just played out.

Police described the new method as 'very worrying' – at least that was the phrase used in public. Behind the scenes, the sentiments were far stronger as officers tackled the utterly barbaric attacks. The only saving grace was that nobody was injured or worse, despite the recklessness of the petrol attacks. The mental scars, however, were immediately evident and it is fair to assume those will never disappear for the guards caught up in those two incidents.

Unusually, in 2009, the same Uddingston bank was again hit by raiders. In March that year, two armed robbers targeted security men, forcing them to open a safe before making away with £100,000 in cash. A getaway driver made up the trio, piloting a silver BMW away from the branch after the 12.45 a.m. attack.

The two attacks featuring petrol were, unfortunately, not isolated. On both sides of the Border, the desperate tactic was employed with alarming regularity as guards were left to rely on their wits to escape with their lives.

In Scotland in 2007, not far from the Uddingston incidents of five years earlier, the same threat was employed during a Post Office robbery in East Kilbride. Again, the guard was doused in petrol and forced to hand over cash. The thief, who police believed was working with a partner, escaped in a stolen Mercedes Coupé. A reward of £5,000 was offered by worried Post Office chiefs after what police described as a 'particularly disturbing attack' in which there was no 'regard whatsoever' for the trauma faced by the victim. The thief made off with a five-figure sum, speeding to Bothwell before dumping the getaway car.

What all of those attacks shared was the common thread of force and threats of violence being used to 'persuade' staff to part with their money. What they didn't involve was an active attempt to gain access using a more direct approach. That was demonstrated better by the audacious gang who struck on 9 April 2003 in Rutherglen. Four men, with their faces masked against the gaze of the security camera network, went to work with a shattering plan – quite literally. For the unsuspecting crew of the Brinks van handling cash from the Bank of Scotland on Stonelaw Road, Burnside, at 1 a.m., the first hint of trouble was when a JCB digger came hurtling towards their vehicle around 100 yards from the branch. The famous machines sport their bright yellow livery for good reason – it is said that, on a construction site, workers are more likely to see a piece of kit in that colour than one painted in any other tone and not least if it is out of the direct line of sight. It is fair to assume the guards on duty that night were not on the lookout for heavy machinery heading in their direction but certainly saw it coming.

The sound of crunching metal and shattering glass that followed was the soundtrack for the episode, as the digger's power and weight were put to use – pinning the security van against a nearby insurance broker's building, taking a parked Ford Fiesta with it, in a scene of carnage on the streets. It was a seven-tonne bright yellow battering ram. Bystanders who witnessed the incredible episode unfolding said it looked to have been a 'well-planned heist'.

The van was shunted off the carriageway on to the pavement, with the digger's bucket providing the battering ram. The heavy metal scoop was then used to smash open the bulletproof glass and leave the driver exposed. It suggested a fair degree of experience since, as anyone who has attempted to operate a digger will admit, the controls are not altogether intuitive. Could there have been practice involved or a dry run?

As the lone member of the gang driving the JCB set about his task there was immediate back-up from two fellow crooks who arrived at the scene in a blue Subaru Impreza. The trio forced their way into the van, threatened staff with guns and then made a quick exit, along with a sum which has been estimated at anywhere between £300,000 and £800,000 in cash. Banks, hit repeatedly by such incidents, were reluctant to publicise the net result.

It was unusual but not unprecedented. In 1985, a security van in Surrey was attacked by a gang using an excavator to cut a hole in the cargo area before making off with hundreds of thousands of pounds.

The terror of having what was, on face value, a strengthened vehicle wrecked by force was one thing for the Rutherglen guards but it got worse as the prospect of sawn-off shotguns being pointed at their heads loomed large, with the guards told they would be shot unless they threw the cash bags out into the open.

A red Vauxhall Vectra, driven by the fourth member of the team, was also used in the raid. Each of the quartet was clad in black and all four had their faces covered by what the victims described as balaclavas or ski masks. They sped off from the bank in the direction of Burnside Road, leaving behind three members of the Brinks staff who were fortunately uninjured but left shaken by their experiences at the hands of their attackers. The Subaru and JCB were recovered for examination and the Vectra was later found torched as the thieves did their best to dispose of lingering evidence in the getaway car. The escape route took them in the direction of Braemar Road in Cathkin, with the Vauxhall dumped in a lane running behind a shopping precinct.

Detective Inspector Gordon McConnell of Rutherglen CID led the public appeal and called for witnesses to come forward. It was becoming a familiar script for detectives, with seven other security van heists in the Central Belt in the space of just six months leading up to the incident.

Slowly the details were pieced together, just as the remnants of the scene were. The first step was to trace the origins of the two vehicles at the centre of the case. The JCB was tracked back to Uddingston Bowling Club from where it had been stolen in the hours leading up to the crime and driven the eight miles to Stonelaw Road ready for the attack.

The Subaru, it transpired, had been taken from a forecourt in Edinburgh 15 days earlier. It was removed from the Calder Motor Company on the capital's Corstorphine Road and stored in the interim, before being wheeled out to provide the rapid transport required by the raiders. The desirability of the Subaru was not surprising, given its purebred rally pedigree and outstanding performance. What its use did do was point to the changing tastes among those involved in Britain's heists. In the 1970s, Scotland Yard famously labelled the humble Ford Transit van as the nation's most wanted, citing the fact that it was used in 95 per cent of bank robberies at the time. Jaguars and Rovers had also been popular whilst fast Fords, such as the Sierra Cosworth, took on the mantle in the 1980s and 90s – with the dubious honour now passed to the likes of Subaru and Mitsubishi as the performance car hierarchy shifts.

The specific car was a far from subtle choice, with the attention-grabbing, high-power model adorned with the registration plate S118ARU, yet nobody appeared to have seen it after it was spirited away from the Calder garage. Police issued a desperate plea for information on the car's whereabouts and also spoke out specifically to one person they believed had key information – a taxi driver who was reported to have been parked and watching as the robbery played out in front of him.

The investigation took police from coast to coast, with the trail from the scene of the car theft leading shortly after the heist to a caravan park in Ayr, where detectives launched a lightning-quick raid, bursting in at midnight and arresting Barry Paul. For Paul, it was the end of the road but, to this day, he remains the only person ever charged in connection with the high-profile and highly lucrative incident. Although Paul, when eventually summoned to appear at the High Court in Glasgow, admitted stealing the JCB and Subaru to order for the gang, it was accepted that he had not been present when the robbery took place. It was also argued in court that he did not know the details of the plans, particularly that guns would be used. After those mitigating circumstances were taken into account, Paul was sentenced to five years in jail by Lord Emslie.

Paul, from Cambuslang, was arrested three weeks after the robbers struck in Rutherglen. In the time between the incident and his arrest, he had been busy. He had spent £6,000 on an Audi and a further £16,480 in cash on a brand-new caravan. His stay in that proved short, rudely interrupted by Strathclyde's finest as they closed the net on one of their prime suspects. A search of the caravan found £1,770 in cash locked inside a newly fitted safe. It remains the only money to have been recovered during the course of the long and winding investigation. Together with the £22,480 Paul was known to have spent, the sum hints at a £25,000 bounty for his part in proceedings.

Work in the cash-in-transit industry has become increasingly perilous. Petrol, guns, diggers and even swords have been used to persuade guards to part with the contents of their vans. It was in May 2012 that a robber armed with a Samurai sword struck again in Uddingston, working with others brandishing baseball bats to liberate £20,000 as security guards transferred the week's canteen takings from the Kwik Fit Insurance office at Tannochside Business Park to their vehicle. It was another black night in a town which has become something of a robbery hot spot, no doubt partly because of its location within easy reach of a motorway network which provides a handy route for disappearing into the night.

According to industry experts, the advent of technology has

posed little deterrent as the three-quarters of a billion pounds transported each day in the UK provides an irresistible lure. One risk management expert in the security van sector said: '[Security vans] are tracked on a permanent basis. We know exactly where [each] vehicle is at any point of time, we know how long it stops for, we know where he's going, what his route is – any deviation of that route we can identify and tell the authorities very quickly exactly where they need to home into.

'You could be looking on a bad week in the UK at 15 attacks. On a less bad week you could be looking at five or six, so the weeks vary – it is partly seasonal, even criminals go on holiday occasionally . . . and then they run out of money and come back.

'If you go to an ATM and it is no longer working you might consider it has run out of money or is no longer working. The likelihood is, in certain parts of the UK, that it hasn't got any money because the crew couldn't get there on the run they were doing that day because they were attacked at a previous site.'

That plague of attacks has led to a weird and wonderful suite of solutions being implemented. A South African firm has recently unveiled one of the more extreme innovations involving a combination of two chemicals being fired into the body of a security van on the command of either threatened crew members or those monitoring CCTV footage back at base. On contact with each other, the two chemicals combine to form a foam barrier which, as it hardens, is resistant to fire and bullets – an instant shield to fend off attackers. That was pioneered by G4S in South Africa although the firm's British experts were not lagging too far behind. In 2010, the UK security specialists revealed a system which used the injection of glue into cash boxes when activated by concerned staff, with the notes inside being rendered useless.

Anyone who has sat behind a security van in traffic will be aware of the collage of warning stickers adorning the vehicles. They are not empty messages – they are part of a real and concerted effort being made to deter would-be attackers. Kevin

O'Connor, risk director with G4S Cash Solutions, said: 'Our tests show that the glue will ensure that an attack on a G4S cashbox will be completely worthless to the perpetrator. This new technology will complement our existing degradations systems of dye and SmartWater.

'Criminals caught following an attack on one of our CIT [cash-in-transit] couriers already face a high probability of being convicted with the aid of SmartWater evidence, which has an impressive 100 percent success rate in securing convictions when used in criminal cases. Glue is the latest in a series of high-tech solutions we have developed to reduce the number of attacks on our CIT crew and vehicles.

'The deployment of glue is another example of a successful partnership between the Met Police and the private sector in developing an effective deterrent against violent attacks on CIT couriers. We continue to work closely with all police forces, trade unions, the government, customers and local communities to develop ways to curtail these attacks.'

The glue was part of a £100-million investment in crime prevention by G4S over a five-year period. Other additions include more heavily armoured vehicles, body armour for staff and the adoption of more high-tech ideas. The partnership with SmartWater Technology was part of that programme, with that firm inventing a system which left any money within a stolen cash box covered in a substance that is invisible to the naked eye. Anyone coming into contact with it would also be marked with a DNA-type code which would remain present for up to six months, enabling police to make a link between unsuspecting criminals and the scene of the crime. G4S makes for an interesting case study, with the company rising to become Britain's market leader in the cash-in-transit business. More than 7,000 employees and 2,000 vehicles, spread across 53 different bases, make the operation tick.

All of the evidence shows that the threat of violence is never far from the surface in security van raids but force is not the only element. It was on 10 October 2011 that the incredible lengths that raiders will go to and the forward planning employed were revealed. It was on that day that Glasgow was hit by raiders in disguise. And not just any disguise – the costume of choice was that of Strathclyde Police, with three men dressed as uniformed officers striking at the NatWest branch in Blythswood Square. And the disguises were not the only unusual facet to the events of that day – the fact that the robbers struck in daylight set it apart from the more usual night-time operations. It was at 10.40 a.m. that the gang made its move, pouncing as the delivery was made. Despite the use of guns, there were no shots fired and nobody was injured. Staff of the bank and the security guard were, understandably, left traumatised.

The police outfits bought the raiders time as they made their move, also adding an all-important element of surprise to their plan. In reality, that surprise lasted only seconds – just as long as it took them to pull out their guns and make their demands.

CCTV footage of the drama was released to the public, coinciding with an announcement that the British Bankers Association was offering a £25,000 reward for information leading to the arrest of the culprits. An e-fit image of one of the suspects was released too, pulled together after scores of witness reports had been collated. All of that pressure and the financial lure did not provide the solution – it was left to detectives to continue the hunt – but it did drag the daylight robbery back into the spotlight.

The footage showed the fake policemen threatening a security guard as he made a cash delivery to the bank. They fled the scene, clutching a stolen cash box, and made off in a silver Mercedes E-Class. The car was last seen heading along Blythswood Street before turning right on to Waterloo Street and then joining the M8's westbound carriageway.

Immediately police launched an intensive and extensive probe, led by Detective Inspector Kate Jamieson of Strathclyde Police. Obtaining footage from all CCTV cameras in the vicinity was a top priority – as was slotting together the observations from witnesses who reported seeing the three 'policemen' in the area during the minutes before they pressed ahead with their heist.

The E-Class used to flee the scene was said to have been driven at speed through the crowded city-centre streets and its erratic journey was something detectives hoped would spark memories among potential witnesses. It was a big beast of a car to pilot through the congested streets but it also had the power and bulk required if a chase had developed and force was needed.

One week later, officers returned to the Blythswood Square bank and set up cordons to stop motorists and pedestrians. It was the latest attempt to pin down evidence that could lead to the robbery gang and to flush out further information. DI Jamieson stated, 'Blythswood Street and Waterloo Street are very busy areas, with both pedestrians and motorists, and I would appeal directly to anyone who may have been in those areas at the time of the incident to come forward to police urgently.'

Tens of thousands of pounds were taken by the culprits. Once again the perils facing those in the cash-in-transit trade on a day-to-day basis were underlined, with the case also emphasising some worrying developments in the business during a period in which companies in every area of commercial life were attempting to tighten the purse strings.

Union officials stepped forward to publicise the fact that, whilst guards had once always worked in pairs as a safety measure, daytime deliveries were, at the time of the NatWest raid, being conducted by lone operatives in an attempt, according to the UK's general trade union GMB at least, to cut costs. It was also suggested that the same reasons were behind the decision not to implement the latest technology, including SmartWater, in the Glasgow area. Cal Waterson, lead officer on the security industry for the GMB, said at the time, 'The problem we have in Glasgow at the moment is the safety back-ups aren't quite as intensive as they are in other parts of the country. Some of the boxes they carry the cash in don't have the explosive dye. The companies are rolling them out as quickly as they can and targeting the worst-attacked areas first.'

Indeed, drivers and crew threatened to strike in the after-math of the JCB attack in Uddingston. It took assurances from bosses that manpower levels would be maintained to avert that action but no amount of promises will ever remove the risk faced by the brave men and women every day of every year on Scotland's streets.

4

A Lasting Impression

The headline in *The Bulletin* said it all – '£35,000 BANK RAID
BAFFLES POLICE'. Officers arrived at an ordinary branch
of the Clydesdale and North of Scotland Bank on an ordinary
high street to find no signs of force and no signs of disruption
but tens of thousands of pounds were missing from the vault.
The gang members responsible were dubbed the 'immaculate
raiders' by journalists, who were as flummoxed as their police
counterparts by what appeared to be the perfect crime.

The scene of this bamboozling heist was the Clydesdale and
North of Scotland Bank at 865 Shettleston Road in Glasgow.
The name provides a hint of the era in question – the 1950s,
a new dawn for the financial services industry in Scotland
but one which was not immune to the problems of old. The
Clydesdale and North of Scotland Bank was born in 1950,
when the Glasgow-based Clydesdale acquired its Northern
counterpart, and existed for just 13 years. In 1963 the institution dropped its extended moniker, becoming simply the
Clydesdale Bank.

In between, it had fallen victim to those apparently 'immaculate' thieves, whose £35,000 haul back then would be worth
nearer £700,000 in today's money. And to get hold of that
sum, it appeared they had used brain rather than brawn. The
quandary for the police and the bank was just how they had
succeeded in breaching security in the dead of night and walking away unchallenged with a small fortune.

Bank robberies, during that period, were far from uncommon. However, the traditional modus operandi involved large

quantities of explosives and a healthy dollop of recklessness. The dynamite technique was far from scientific and, as a result, not entirely effective. It was also less than subtle, leading to a more than reasonable chance of being caught in the act.

What had occurred in Shettleston was different to the norm and that presented new challenges for a City of Glasgow Police force which was much more familiar with picking through the wreckage left behind by the safe-blowing fraternity than combing a pristine crime scene offering no visible clues. The Clydesdale may have gone on to pioneer the use of the automatic teller machine (ATM) in the 1970s, but in the 1950s it had yet to discover the benefits of the CCTV camera.

That left Detective Inspector Donald Campbell, of the city's Eastern CID, to begin piecing together evidence and painting his own picture of events leading up to the disappearance of the cash. He was one of Glasgow's most respected officers, something of a rising star in the force, and destined to earn subsequent promotion. It was Campbell who had been tasked with heading up the Shettleston investigation and he arrived at the start of a fingertip search of the premises, at the heart of a bustling east-end community. Today, the Clydesdale Bank is a modern building standing on the site of what, in 1959, had been a traditional set-up, with the branch at ground floor and residential flats above. A mix of shops and pubs surrounded it, with the branch sitting on a busy thoroughfare and certainly not hidden from prying eyes. So how did somebody succeed in walking in and walking back out again with £35,000?

The police investigation began early on 30 April 1959. It had been quickly convened at the Shettleston Road branch after a telephone call from startled staff who had reported for duty and discovered the money was missing. Officers and bank staff remained at the branch well into the evening as they searched for explanations. The crime scene was closely scrutinised, with fingerprint experts quickly collating evidence for examination at Glasgow's police labs.

The Shettleston branch was no stranger to incident. Just two months earlier, a quick-thinking teller had swept bundles of cash from the counter and on to the floor to foil a young man's attempts to swipe the cash. The year before a window had been smashed with a brick and thieves reached in to lift £200 in cash. However, the April raid was in a whole new league to those earlier attempts and it happened on the watch of a rookie as the manager of the branch had only been in place for three weeks when the thieves struck. He and his four colleagues, all men, arrived for work on a Tuesday morning to be greeted by a stomach-churning realisation.

Interviews with staff ascertained that the money had been securely stored in the bank's main vault when the branch was closed for the evening. When they arrived the following morning, it had vanished. When the employees turned up, they found the wooden double-front doors intact and there was no damage to the three rear windows or the protective grilles guarding them. Inside, the safe door was closed but not locked. The contents were gone but the keys which provided access to the vault had not been disturbed and remained locked away where they always sat. There was no sign of any use of explosives or force of any description.

There were no immediate suspects and DI Campbell admitted on the day, 'It's a mystery. We still don't know how many men were involved or the time when the raid took place.'

Chief Detective Superintendent Robert Colquhoun, head of Glasgow's CID, was also on the scene along with other high-ranking officers as the force threw resources at the headline-grabbing affair. A door-to-door operation was launched in the hope of unearthing eyewitness information – but even those living in flats directly above the bank hadn't heard or seen a thing. Not only were the raiders immaculate, they were also quiet.

Attention focused intently on the safe itself. It was an old unit, manufactured in 1910, but there was no reason to suggest age had anything to do with the apparent ease with which it had been breached. It had been made by Milner, one of the most respected names in the industry. Thomas Milner had founded the company in 1814 and it rapidly expanded – the brand was favoured by many of the leading banks and Milner safes were even said to have been used on the *Titanic*. The company would put on dramatic public shows, testing their models against raging fires and even gunpowder in front of awestruck audiences. One such occasion ended in tragedy, when a boy in the audience was struck by shrapnel from the demonstration and died from his injuries.

Milner was eventually swallowed up by Chubb in the 1960s but elements of the firm's technology were still being utilised right up to the 1990s so there was no question that it could have been considered outmoded back in 1959. The List 5 model, the one fitted at Shettleston, was drill resistant with its metal 'sandwich' design door and had three key locks running down its door. Three-way bolt work was the other feature which helped increase resistance to explosives, typically rendering the door seized shut if one of those bolts was blown. On face value, it appeared almost impenetrable to even the most forceful attack but that clearly hadn't been the case. Police in Glasgow quickly came to the only logical conclusion that the locks had been compromised and the realisation caused the Clydesdale and North of Scotland Bank to sit up and take notice.

In the aftermath, all of the organisation's safes were fitted with keyless combination locks with spy-proof dials. Beyond that, an even more secure breed of 'time-lock' protection was then fitted as precautions were taken to new levels – all of which was great for the future but it did nothing to deal with the present or to reunite the bankers with their missing money.

As the investigation at Shettleston took shape, the five members of staff faced an intense grilling from detectives. It became apparent early on in the process that they would hold the answers to many of the questions surrounding the heist. One thing that was causing concern was the timing of the robbery. The thieves had struck on a day when the bank was cash-laden, primed and ready to deal with the end of month payroll for the district's teachers. Those wages were processed through the Shettleston branch at the same time each month and it quickly became clear that the idea of inside information being used to tip off the raiders was at the forefront of the minds of the detectives.

With that idea under consideration, the internal arrangements then came under particular scrutiny. The manager outlined the present system in place to ensure security of the cash safe. No member of staff should have had access to all three keys at one time; the manager would have to be notified when his key was required and subsequently know each and every time the vault was opened. However, lapses in that procedure were also disclosed by staff at the branch. Police were told that, given the busy nature of the operation and the bond of trust between the close-knit team, there were occasions when keys were left on top of the safe or even in the locks themselves. It was the first sign of cracks within the system – but all three of those keys had been accounted for at the time of the incident so it still did not explain the missing cash.

The fabric of the building, in particular the mortise lock on the solid wooden front doors, also fell under the spotlight. With the aid of specialists, police were able to ascertain that it was not a fail-safe set-up. In fact, master keys for the particular model of lock existed and not all of them were far from the scene of the crime. In time, it was discovered by the team investigating the raid that, amongst others, the master key for a synagogue in Edinburgh worked equally well in the Shettleston bank lock. It was just another quirk in the tale, as the security issues began to unravel.

The potential for a dummy key to have been used to gain access to the branch was clear but officers came to the conclusion that the only possible explanation for the safe being cracked was that it had been an inside job. Since the first lock was invented until modern times, one fact remains true – a key cannot be copied without there first having been access to the original.

Douglas Campbell, owner of Kelvin Lock and Safe in Glasgow, is a member of the Master Locksmiths Association. He admits the tools of his trade have not changed dramatically since the Shettleston heist in the 1950s and many of the techniques remain relevant to those with a legitimate cause to cut keys. Campbell told me: 'Locking has improved over the years but the principles remain the same. Some of the features from the case in the 50s are not totally outdated – I've had people come to me with impressions of a key they have made in a bar of soap because they only have one at home and that's in use. It is possible to create a key using a mould like that but there does tend to be a fair bit of trial and error involved. It would need to be someone with the expertise to make the key, so a locksmith would have to be involved.

'It certainly isn't impossible, whether using soap or Plasticine as the basis for the mould, but the bottom line in any incident like that is it has to be an inside job. You have to have the original key to be able to make the impression and create the mould so it is a relatively easy one to investigate. Quite often, down through the years, you would find people would cause damage to a safe to give the impression that force had been used rather than keys but you can always tell when that has been the case. Anyone with a good knowledge of the trade would be able to spot that almost instantly.

'Much depends on the type of lock and the age of that lock. It would be far easier to make a copy of a key in that way if it was for a safe manufactured in the late 1800s or early part of the 20th century. If you move forward to the 1970s and 80s, things had moved on by then – some of the locks manufactured by the likes of Chubb, Chatwood and Wolfshead in that particular period were like works of art, so intricate and consequently very secure.

'Even before then there was a great pride taken by the major firms in how well made their locks were. Chubb and Brahma would have great competitions in which they would put forward what they described as the 'unpickable' lock. In truth, any lock can be picked if you have the skill, the time and the patience to do it. In saying that, there are people out there who can pick modern locks but wouldn't be able to get past one of the older, more complex locks.

'I don't think I will see the day in my lifetime when the

traditional lock becomes redundant. Certainly electronics, particularly in safes, are becoming more prominent and the likes of fingerprint recognition take it to a new level completely. But there is still something reassuring about having a key in your pocket – if you have a push-button lock or a coded system there is always the possibility something could malfunction or somebody could simply get lucky and guess the right numbers.'

Campbell is aware of the systems the various banks had in place to make their safes secure but, as he is quick to point out, there is a long history of trying to stay ahead of criminals and it has not always been successful. He told me: 'Since the first lock was invented, people have been trying to make them tamper-proof – some systems have been more successful than others. The Egyptians would fit their locks in a recess in the wall so whoever was using it had to put their hand in and operate the lock. If the wrong key was used, a guillotine would drop and they would lose their hand – I can't imagine that worked too well. What if you had just ended up with a faulty key?

'The two-key system operated during that era was effective in theory as you would need two people to open the safe. Where it fell down was if things got busy and both keys were handed over or, worse than that, if the safe was left sitting open all day. I believe that did happen in some instances.'

In his professional life, Campbell has had to deal with the aftermath of some elaborate attempts to break into safes and has no time for those who have made it their life's work to try to get the better of security systems. He said: 'There has always been a habit of glamorising safe breakers. Johnny Ramensky was one who was always spoken about but he was always getting caught. Where was the sense in that? Generally, you find they always got caught in the end, whether that was because they started spending money and drawing attention to themselves or because they made mistakes that led police to them.

'Some of the schemes nowadays are incredible. I've been to petrol stations that have used underfloor safes where staff simply deposit capsules of cash in through a tube – criminals have broken in and poured lemonade and anything else they

can get their hands on into the safe to try and make the capsules bob up to the surface and out. I've never seen it work but
I have had to deal with the clean-up operation afterwards. The
world has changed though. Whereas once criminals would take
the time to try and break into safes, today they are far more
likely to go in with guns and knives. It is all brute force and
ignorance.'

In contrast, there was no need for force in the Shettleston
heist of 1959. Each of the five members of staff were pushed
and probed when it became clear inside help would have been
required but they all appeared to be diligent and dedicated
members of the team. Until, eventually, one of that group
cracked. That man was William Rae, an 18-year-old apprentice
teller. He did not appear to have the hallmarks of a criminal
mastermind. Rather, he was a fresh-faced, red-haired teenager
who, when the investigation was launched, hadn't created as
much as a ripple of suspicion. However, when faced with the
headline-hogging reality of what had happened, Rae admitted his part in the operation. It took two weeks for detectives
to break his resistance but, when they did, some staggering
insights into what had been a protracted and carefully considered plot emerged.

Most astonishing of all was that the bank had been breached
not once but twice. On the first occasion, the 'immaculate
raiders' had been so careful that their sortie hadn't even been
noticed by management. They had entered in the dead of night
in February 1959 but, upon discovering less money than they
would have liked in the safe, they exited without taking a penny
and resolved to return when the profit was likely to be greater.
And they did, coming back with a vengeance on 29 April to
escape with their £35,000 haul.

It took near enough two months for Glasgow's finest to
crack the case, which proved more difficult than it had been for
the robbers to crack the safe. With Rae opting to turn Queen's
evidence and assist the authorities in bringing his cohorts to
justice, the story still had to be corroborated and the jigsaw
pieced together bit by bit. Eventually, in June 1959, police

made their move and the big breakthrough came to pass. Two houses in the city were raided in quick succession – the first on Great Western Road and the second in Castlemilk – and four men and a woman were arrested in connection with the Shettleston raid and taken to the Tobago Street police station. There, Samuel Mackay, Alexander Gray, Patrick Rice, Jean Rice and Hugh Mannion were charged with breaking into the branch on 29 April, working with Rae to gain access, and stealing £38,789.

Police had never considered Rae to be the driving force – instead, it transpired that Alexander Gray had been the brains behind the lucrative operation. Gray was a well-known Shettleston face, operating a bookmaker's business and gambling club near to the bank he targeted in the biggest gamble of his life. When the case against the accused was called at the High Court in Glasgow in October 1959, the extent of Gray's scheming was revealed.

Rae had been a visitor to Gray's premises on Shettleston Road and Gray had been a customer at the bank as he changed coins into notes. The pair had struck up conversations from day to day. In time, Rae had asked Gray about the possibility of part-time work with him to supplement his Clydesdale wage but the reply he got was not what he had been expecting. Rather than offering employment, Gray revealed he wanted to rob a bank – and not just any bank, but Rae's bank. The teenager, who travelled to his day job from his home in nearby Carntyne, thought the businessman was joking but soon discovered he was deadly serious.

A role in a major heist was not quite what the 18-year-old had in mind when he went in search of extra income and he had not initially succumbed. The 'negotiation' process was aided by a steady flow of alcohol, with Gray grooming his young target during a drinking session which ran long into the night. They started off at Cairns on Miller Street, a bar which today is a popular modern spot with an intriguing past. It was at Cairns, one of Glasgow's oldest pubs, that the seeds for the Shettleston raid were sown in 1959. The party moved on to

Sloans in the Argyll Arcade, another old favourite on the city's pub and restaurant scene, and Rae admitted he remembered little of the events of that evening. What wasn't in dispute was that, during the course of that night, his life changed forever, as he became embroiled in something which surely could not have been further from his mind when he reported for his first day's work at the bank just over a year earlier.

His reward was to be £100 upfront – a reasonable sum for a teenager in the 1950s – as well as a share of the eventual proceeds. It was reported the split could even be as high as 50 per cent for Rae. Shortly after Rae had agreed to play a part in Gray's enterprise, the ringleader's plan began to take shape. He presented his rookie sidekick with a chrome soap dish which had been packed with Plasticine. In a throwback to a black-and-white prisoner-of-war camp or jailbreak movie plot, Rae was ordered to make imprints of the safe keys and smuggle them out of the bank. Unfortunately, it wasn't quite as simple as it was made to appear on the silver screen. Rae was able to take advantage of the occasional lapses in the bank system, with stolen moments with the safe keys enabling him to make prints in the Plasticine, but the end results were flawed. Time after time, 'false' keys were cut using the impressions as a mould but, time and time again, when Rae was given the new keys to try, they did not open the vault.

It was a twist of fortune which allowed a solution to be found. When a bank colleague left to go on annual leave, he passed on his set of keys to the apprentice teller Rae. That gave him the opportunity to sneak those keys out of the bank during breaks and to ferret them away to Gray – rendezvousing in a local baker's shop – for the more experienced criminal hands to have a try. Still it was not an instant success. Rae was given nine keys to try as a result of the renewed attempts but just one of those turned a lock on the safe and, even then, only partially. What had started with great expectation had turned into apparent folly.

With frustration building, Gray decided to enlist the services of William Mercer – a foreman joiner with experience of working with locks. Mercer attempted to adjust the set of false keys which had been fashioned but conceded defeat and told his associates that he would need the originals to start from scratch with. Rae came good, the keys were provided and the job was eventually done. A set of working copies was created and Gray's crew had access to the vault. They also had access to the bank building itself – a key for the mortise lock on the front door was found in Gray's possession. They were all the tools the gang required to make their move and pull off the immaculate raid.

The plot did not end there, however. Realising that the finger of blame would immediately point to members of the branch staff and perhaps sensing Rae's vulnerability to police pressure, Gray decided he needed to disguise the roots of the operation. He sought out an experienced safe blower who was tasked with entering the bank after the money had safely been removed and using explosives to hide the fact the robbers had gained entry with keys. That element of the blueprint had to be ripped up when he turned up at the allotted time to discover the bank's cleaner had reported for duty that evening, rather than in the morning as was the usual routine. He had no option but to walk away, leaving behind the crime scene in unaltered form, as well as thousands of pounds which he was due to pick up as payment.

The other members of the gang worked hard to ensure they had alibis in place, making sure they were seen and heard at various locations in the city centre and at Glasgow Airport. Every angle was covered – the only thing they could not take care of was ensuring the secrets of the raid stayed within the circle of trust.

It was late in June 1959 that it all came to a head with the five arrests. The indictment against Alexander Gray, Patrick Rice, Jean Rice and Hugh Mannion alleged that they carried out the robbery while acting with William Rae and Samuel 'Dandy' McKay – who was still at large at the time of the eventual trial after escaping from the hospital wing of Barlinnie shortly after his initial arrest. It was another twist in an eventful story.

McKay was described in *Evening Times* reports of the time as a 'big-time gambler, owner of two betting clubs' and a 'high-living fugitive from justice'. Following his arrest, he had attempted to do a deal with police, telling detectives that, if they let him go free, he would lead them to £30,000 of the missing cash within two days. It did not work and he reverted to plan B – hatching his escape arrangements with outside help.

Just as the Plasticine plot was akin to something from a film script, so too was McKay's escape. Ropes were used to allow him to abseil from the prison grounds, after the bars had been removed from the window by sawing through the metal. It is believed he fled first to Canada and also spent time in the US before returning, via Glasgow and London, to build a new life in Ireland with his wife and two young children. He used an assumed name and was said by neighbours to lead a quiet life as a doting dad. That happily-ever-after script was ripped up when, in the summer of 1960, ten detectives surrounded the bungalow he had bought in a village near Dublin and he surrendered without a fight to face the music back in Scotland.

Around a year prior to his arrest, there had been a fresh impetus in the case when £5,000 of the stolen cash was recovered when a member of the public surrendered an attaché case packed with the money after mistakenly being handed it at the left luggage desk at St Enoch Station. Detectives kept watch on the left luggage department and soon identified another individual who claimed he had received a case in error. Matching the two together, they swooped to question that second man. Samuel McKay's brother, John McKay, was charged with resetting £5,175 from the alleged haul. Like his fellow accused, he denied the charge levelled against him and the trial began in October 1959.

Rae turned Queen's evidence ahead of the trial and stood in the dock to reveal the intimate detail of every stage of the plan. At the end of the High Court trial there was a 10-year prison sentence for Gray, with his three fellow accused – Patrick Rice, Jean Rice and Hugh Mannion – acquitted.

Gray, cutting a stocky figure in the dock, gave evidence in

his own defence, claiming he had been framed and that police were desperate to pin responsibility for the heist on him. He also suggested the fact Samuel McKay was on the run had an influence on witnesses, insinuating they would have been frightened of recrimination if they had implicated the absentee. He said he 'presumed' that Rae had been 'terrorised' by McKay and this had shaped the evidence Rae had given during the court proceedings.

A key fitting the front door of the Shettleston bank had been found in a drawer in Gray's home but he was relaxed in his explanation, insisting he knew nothing about it and he must have inherited the key when he moved into the property a year earlier. Either that, he said, or it was one of the many keys and locks he had collected during 15 years as a joiner. Despite his best attempts, the jury were not convinced and found him guilty.

John McKay was jailed for three years. Samuel McKay was eventually sentenced to eight years in prison for his part in the robbery plus a further two years for his initial escape from Barlinnie.

There was a footnote to the whole episode. The publicity at the time of the court case and during the investigation around the fact the crew responsible for the robbery had used 'false' keys to gain access, to both the building and the vault, appeared to have sparked something of a trend. The Shettleston raid marked the start of a spate of similar incidents in the city in the middle part of 1959. In June, two months after the first attack, the British Linen Bank branch on the Gallowgate was hit when thieves using false keys walked in and promptly attempted to blow open the safes. They failed and fled empty-handed.

Days later, the Royal Bank of Scotland was on the receiving end – this time at Charing Cross. Again false keys were the order of the day but the modus operandi varied somewhat in that it was not the bank branch which was unlocked. Instead, the gang used their specially created key to open a dentist's surgery located above the RBS premises, cut their way through the roof and dropped 15 feet by rope into the heart of the bank. After failing to blast open the main safe, they turned their attention to the vault containing the night deposits and succeeded in making away with thousands of pounds in cash. The haul was described as 'infinitesimal' in comparison to what it could have been if the plan had been 100 per cent successful but police still pointed towards the expertise of the plotting and elements of the execution as they began their hunt for the culprits in what was the latest in a series of episodes. As one chapter closed with the conclusion of the Shettleston case, many more opened for Glasgow's boys in blue.

5

The First Rule of Robbery

Don't panic. If there's one motto writ large in the bank robber's handbook, that must surely be it. For those responsible for what at the time was Scotland's biggest cash heist, the maxim was taken to a whole new level.

After pulling off an armed raid at a Glasgow branch of the Clydesdale Bank in 1972, the three-man team were the model of composure. They walked to their parked getaway car – no sign of a jog, let alone a sprint – and sat, together with their £65,000 haul, in their stolen Ford Zephyr for a few moments before starting the engine, signalling and making their exit into the flow of traffic in an orderly fashion.

Disappearing into the distance in their rear-view mirror was the Clydesdale's Hillington branch, part of the fabric of a sprawling industrial estate. Quite importantly for the driver and passenger in the maroon-coloured Ford, it was very well placed for accessing the M8 motorway.

It was around 3 p.m. when they struck – closing time for the bank staff. After a busy Tuesday, the cash drawers and vaults were full of notes and coins collected during the course of the working day and that amount had been bolstered by a large delivery of sterling earlier that day. The employees were subjected to a terrifying ordeal by the masked trio, whose sense of calm was chilling. The first robber, thought to be between 25 and 30 years of age, had fair hair, wore a cream overcoat and spoke with a Scottish accent. The second, said to be around 25 with dark hair, wore denim clothing or a boiler suit with a cream balaclava. The third, who is thought to have remained in the car throughout, was never properly seen by witnesses. Neither of the pair who entered the bank was particularly tall or particularly powerful but they didn't need to be because of the weaponry which accompanied them as they set about their work. It marked them out as professionals rather than opportunistic amateurs and made it all the more important that they were apprehended sooner rather than later.

Once inside the building, they produced a shotgun and a pistol or revolver, threatening tellers and quickly getting their hands on the huge sum of money which was being held in the branch. The culprits forced two of the tellers and two female customers to stare down the barrel of the shotgun as they demonstrated steely aggression in their quest for a profitable afternoon. The warning barked out was simple: 'If everyone behaves, no one will get hurt.' A bag was thrown onto the bank's counter with instructions for the tellers to fill it. They stuffed the money in bundles of £20, £10, £5 and £1 notes into a brown canvas holdall and handed it over to the robbers who then strolled out into the afternoon sunshine.

The staff quickly called in police and had to go through the incident blow by blow again as they gave the initial statements to set the investigation rolling – a traumatic experience relived as they outlined the fear they felt when faced with the gun-toting raiders. A police guard was put in place at the branch as officers left nothing to chance whilst employees and witnesses were quizzed inside – all of whom were said to have been left badly shaken.

As officers took those statements at Hillington, colleagues in the Renfrewshire and Bute force moved quickly to throw up cordons all around the area as they sought the Ford seen driving away from the bank in the aftermath of the robbery. It was found within hours, abandoned at nearby Glasgow Airport – posing two immediate questions. How had the driver and passengers made it through the police roadblocks? And had the trio continued their getaway by air rather than road? The prospect added an intriguing new dimension as the possibility of an international element to the mystery was considered and assistance from Interpol was put on the agenda. Police poured into the vicinity of the airport. The terminal building was targeted, passengers waiting to board planes were questioned and the surrounding offices and cargo units were also searched in the hope of catching the raiders red-handed.

Of course, in 1972, the airport was nothing like the hub we know today. It had only opened six years previously and handled 1.5 million passengers in its first year. Today, that figure would be surpassed in just three months. By the 1970s, it was a busier place, with airlines such as Laker, Tarom, Britannia, British Midland, Iberia and Channel running flights to popular destinations in Europe, so a far-flung getaway destination was certainly possible.

The bank in question's location had perhaps been one of the key elements for the raiders. The sprawling 320-acre Hillington site holds the distinction of being Scotland's first ever industrial estate, officially opened in 1938 after being built in an attempt to get the country's economy moving again after the downturn of the 30s. Situated just four miles from the city on land between Renfrew Road and Paisley Road, south of the M8, the Renfrewshire site quickly won favour with a number of leading firms, including Rolls Royce, as a manufacturing base, and remained buoyant after its initial success. Infrastructure sprang up – from parks and garden areas for workers to make use of to first-aid facilities and food outlets. The banks also saw an opportunity and the Clydesdale moved in to take advantage of a captive market. Indeed, the firm remained active for decades, moving out of the Queen Elizabeth Avenue branch in 1979 to take occupancy of a new purpose-built building nearby on another Hillington site.

Despite turbulent economic times throughout Hillington's lifespan, it has remained a constant on the Glasgow business and industrial landscape. Today it is classed as Scotland's largest industrial estate, with tenants in every industry from bed manufacture to construction and coffee distribution. Diversity has always been at the heart of the commercial park and providing banking facilities was important – particularly in the days before online transactions became commonplace and payroll was also handled in cash rather than through transfers.

As well as location, the timing was also interesting. The raiders had chosen the eve of one of the city's great sporting occasions to carry out their attack. Rangers and thousands of the club's supporters were already in Barcelona for the European Cup Winners' Cup Final appearance against Moscow Dynamo, which was to be played the day after the Hillington raid. Hundreds of Rangers fans were flying out from Glasgow Airport to follow their team on the day of the bank raid and they were inevitably among those stopped and questioned by the police in the terminal. Was it coincidence that the cup final week had been chosen or did the planning extend to picking a time at which attention across Glasgow was focussing on the looming Nou Camp encounter? If they thought the football spectacle would ensure publicity of the raid was kept to a minimum, they were wrong.

Despite the distractions of Rangers' exploits, the Hillington heist was still front-page news with the *Evening Times* headline, 'REWARD OUT FOR RAIDERS'. The story related to the Clydesdale's offer of a 10 per cent bounty on any cash recovered during the course of the investigation, with bank chiefs clearly hoping their loss could be mitigated with a little bit of financial pressure. *The Glasgow Herald* hit the newsstands with '£63,000 HAUL FROM SHOTGUN RAID ON BANK' – a reference to the initial estimate of the sum involved. That was later adjusted upwards to exactly £65,704.34 after a thorough audit.

The publicity was designed to encourage further input to the police probe, although well-meaning witnesses had, in fact, hindered the earliest stages of the investigation. Within minutes of the raid, police had been told that two men and two women had been seen leaving in a green car – a vehicle initially sought by officers, then quickly eliminated as more information began to filter through. Vital time was spent following up that line of inquiry, although detectives were at pains to point out that the initial tip-off was well intentioned rather than malicious.

On 25 June 1974, more than two years after the heist, the first sign of a breakthrough was made public when it was revealed that Robert Ross had been arrested in connection with the incident. Aged 40 at the time, he was described as a prisoner in Barlinnie when he made his first court appearance in relation to the Hillington robbery. Ross was jailed for nine years for his part in the crime, as well as for taking part in an even bigger raid on the Whiteinch branch of the Clydesdale in Glasgow in 1974.

Ross was not the main attraction for police – that role fell to a familiar face by the name of James Crosbie. In September 1974, the incredible story was played out in the High Court in Edinburgh as Crosbie, aged 37 at that time, appeared in the dock charged with masterminding three robberies which had netted in excess of £170,000. Hillington was the first of those major crimes. The second was the Whiteinch heist in which £87,000 was stolen – the largest-ever bank robbery in Scotland at that time – and the third was in Edinburgh, again in 1974, when more than £17,000 was grabbed in an attack on the Royal Bank of Scotland branch on Gorgie Road.

Crosbie's punishment was a 20-year prison sentence, more than double that of his accomplice, although it was clear Ross had a vital role to play. He had been employed as a messenger at the Clydesdale bank's head office in Glasgow and was able to gain the inside information which aided the carefully considered planning of both the Hillington and Whiteinch operations. He had also accompanied Crosbie when the Hillington raid was carried out, a trusted ally for the more experienced of the two criminals as they plotted their get-rich-quick schemes.

The second of the three Crosbie raids was the most alarming for those on his trail. He had struck at the Clydesdale's Whiteinch branch, on Dumbarton Road, on 30 April 1974 and arrived armed with a pistol. Two shots rang out inside the building as the team threatened staff and got their hands on

£87,000 in cash. That money had been delivered just moments earlier and had not yet been placed in the vault. This led detectives at the time to claim the raiders must have struck lucky. They described the timing as a 'fluke' despite admitting there was a possibility of inside information being put to use.

After the burst of shots inside the bank, a further bullet was fired from the getaway car, missing a passer-by, yet the contention from the defendant in court was that those had all been accidental. The threat posed by guns was one thing but, when they began to be fired in anger, it put a completely different complexion on the crime. Not that all of the witnesses felt threatened – far from it, in fact.

Thomas Timms, aged 61 at the time, was standing outside the branch at the time of the mid-morning raid. He told reporters at the time: 'It was like the Keystone Cops. I heard shots coming from inside the building. Then a tall man carrying a shotgun came running out and got into a car only a few yards from me in Glendore Street. A smaller man backed out of the bank door firing into the building as he came out into the street.

'He was carrying a case under one arm. The magazine fell out of his gun as he ran towards the car and he had to stop to pick it up. He put it back, then aimed the gun at me and fired in my direction. I wasn't hit, even though he was only a few yards away. He had to bang on the back of the car as it started to move off. Then he fired a shot at it and his partner let him in. The car swung round into Dumbarton Road and made off. At first I thought they were making a film – it was like *Z-Cars* or the Keystone Cops.'

Almost exactly five years later, the same branch of the Clydesdale was hit again when three shotgun-wielding robbers burst in and once again threatened staff. That gang made their escape with just £2,500 in a raid in which the proceeds did not match the violent means. They fled in a stolen red Ford Cortina driven by a fourth member of their crew, with the car later found abandoned in Yoker, and disappeared into the busy city streetscape of Glasgow to set another challenge for the local constabulary. Crosbie was not involved in that one.

There was an added twist to the story of the getaway in the 1974 heist. After fleeing in a car, the raiders transferred to bicycles, which had been discreetly parked approximately a mile away at Broomhill Lane, and pedalled off into the distance. In the car, they had left behind a pair of raincoats and a wig, part of the disguise used during the raid. Is it possible they could have been aware of the fact that Whiteinch was a branch equipped with a security camera? After collecting his bike, Crosbie, with a rucksack on his back, was said to have taken with him the lion's share of the proceeds of that afternoon's action. The use of bikes was just another nod towards the deep thinking that went into each of the raids, with every avenue explored in the fine tuning of the planning.

It was claimed that Crosbie had used his pilot's licence during the Hillington episode, although not directly. He had obtained the permit after taking flying lessons and was said to have used it as a badge of respectability, coupled with dapper clothes, to drive through a police cordon near to the airport during his getaway. It was clever, elaborate and had all the hallmarks of the type of confidence which became a trademark for a man who, at one stage, was Scotland's most wanted. It appeared he thrived on the execution of his blueprints as much as he did on the proceeds.

Some of the money from the £170,000 spree was recovered but the majority was not. Ross had been paid £7,000 for his efforts but Crosbie secured the most. He was said to have spent freely after the initial Hillington heist, and by the time the net closed in around him there was only £48,246 for the authorities to reclaim. Taking into account the payment to Ross, it left a gap of £114,754 which was never filled. Crosbie had been quick to admit his guilt but less speedy to lead police to the missing money.

It was the discovery of some of the cash which led to Crosbie's arrest in the first instance. Having stashed around £40,000 in a safe house, the notes were discovered by a friend of the householder's daughter and eventually police were alerted. The tangled web began to unravel and the prime suspect for the two Glasgow bank raids was arrested. But that was not where the story ended. Enlisting the help of renowned Glasgow solicitor Joe Beltrami, Crosbie was incredibly granted bail and allowed to walk from the court pending the next stage of the action against him. It was an invitation he simply could not ignore and the robber promptly disappeared without a trace. It later transpired he had been hiding out in Falkirk and, as funds began to run low, he reverted to type and got hold of a gun to enable him to carry out his next attack. The artful dodger was seeking funds to enable him to skip the country and, having perhaps exhausted opportunities in Glasgow, he turned his attention to Edinburgh and the Royal Bank of Scotland branch at Gorgie. Having scouted out the target, everything went to plan. It was just an error in delaying too long which cost him dear.

Crosbie was apprehended by quick-thinking police in the capital after they recognised him in the street the day after his exploits. He had at his side a holdall packed with £20,000 which he had earmarked to help him start a new life, possibly abroad, away from the prospect of another prison term. The officers in question were, in fact, Glasgow-based but had been through on the east coast on other police business when they ran into their force's old adversary on unfamiliar territory and struck it lucky on the day in question.

At the High Court in Edinburgh, Lord Robertson was damning during his sentencing address. He said, 'James Crosbie, you are nothing more than a cold, calculating scoundrel whom I consider to be the most dangerous man in Scotland and, indeed, a threat to the very fabric of our society.'

Crosbie had been no stranger to the boys in blue. A Glaswegian born and bred, he already had 14 convictions by the time the three major bank jobs were added to his record. Those went as far back as 1950 and had led to a spell in borstal when he was a young man growing up in Springburn. Subsequent prison sentences for a range of offences including housebreaking and the reset of stolen property followed. Crosbie first made the news as an 18-year-old when his escape from Glasgow Sheriff

Court was reported in *The Bulletin,* with the teenager exiting through a toilet window as he awaited an appearance on fraud charges. He had been accused of obtaining a car by deception but clearly did not fancy hanging around to discover the court's view on that particular deed.

His passion for risk taking saw him drift into dubious company. As he admitted himself in an interview in later life, 'There was all sorts of things going on in London in those days and it was easy to get mixed up in it all. I never really did anything violent though.'

When Crosbie was jailed for three and a half years for conspiracy to rob, his time in Verne Prison in Dorset brought him to the attention of the Kray Twins. He was asked to make counterfeit driving licences for Britain's most feared gangsters – if nothing else, this was an endorsement of his standing in the league of criminal 'talents'.

He had also had legitimate employment in his life, first as an electrician in London and then as a businessman in his own right back in Glasgow. He was successful and did not need to rob banks to survive but appeared to be driven by the thrill of it all.

Others appeared ready to follow Crosbie's lead. Just 18 months after the Clydesdale raid, another bank on the Hillington estate was targeted by thugs. This time, the gang of four came armed with pickaxe handles and lay in wait for a payroll run from the Royal Bank of Scotland branch to the nearby Personna blade factory. A clerk was bundled to the ground and robbed of £7,000 in cash, with the accompanying driver also threatened during the incident in October 1973. The quartet fled the scene in a van before continuing their getaway in a red Volkswagen car which had been parked close by.

In 1989, by which time the branch was located in a new building, the Clydesdale in Hillington was again subjected to unwanted attention when armed robbers ambushed a Securicor delivery and made off with £7,000. One of the robbers fired a gun in the air and the other hit the guard on the legs with a hammer before making their getaway in a red Ford Escort, which was found abandoned near a footbridge over the M8 at Cocklesloan. It was not quite in the same league as Crosbie and his elite crew but definitely following in their footsteps.

The 1980s' incident was unusual but in the 1970s a spate of bank robberies in Glasgow was to touch the consciousness of the public. Among the suggestions from concerned Glaswegians at the time, aired through the forum of the city's newspaper letters columns, was that each bank branch could be equipped with a trained marksman to work incognito among its staff and be primed and ready to swing into action in the event of an armed raid. It was an extreme reaction but a measure of how perturbed some were by the alarming number of incidents being recorded across Strathclyde. The deterrent of a prison sentence, it was said, was not enough to prevent repeats.

Certainly, in the case of Crosbie, jail was not enough to keep him on the straight and narrow. In 1996, he was caught attempting to smuggle cannabis worth £250,000 at Birmingham Airport and sentenced to four years. In 2000, back on the outside, he was again caught up in a drugs case when he was captured attempting to board a ship destined for Iceland whilst laden with cannabis. This time he was jailed for eight years but was released in 2005 and vowed to settle down as a family man. That included indulging in his new-found passion for writing – a talent he had explored whilst in prison and one that had won praise from judges of the Koestler Awards, which had been established to celebrate the art of prisoners.

A winner of Koestler Awards, he went on to sit on the Koestler Trust judging panel alongside figures such as poet Douglas Dunn, also a former professor of English at St Andrews University, and Sarah Saunders of the National Galleries of Scotland. It was a mark of how much his life had changed during his time inside and, in many ways, demonstrated how the awards helped to rehabilitate those who embraced the arts world whilst serving sentences in Scotland's prisons. For

Crosbie, it sparked a passion for the keyboard which brought him attention for all the right reasons.

Among the books he has had published are accounts of his own criminal enterprises, including the Glasgow bank raids, as well as a collection of stories about the lighter side of life in Peterhead prison. His early efforts gained positive reviews from those who read them but Crosbie did not restrict himself to autobiographical or factual titles. In 2009, his first attempt at fiction, *Ashanti Gold*, was published. The novel was set in Ghana and it stemmed from his experiences of life in the African country, where he spent time in the 1960s, as well as from his time in Nigeria whilst working in the cocoa trade. Those were just two more stops on an eventful journey in which the Glaswegian also rubbed shoulders with some of Britain's most notorious gangsters.

At the time of *Ashanti Gold*'s launch, Crosbie revealed in an interview: 'The story is about 80 per cent truth and 20 per cent fiction. I lived in Ghana in the early Sixties and I went to see the diamond fields and gold mines. I always wondered, especially when I was at the gold mines, how they could be robbed. So while the book is based on a lot of my own experiences of Ghana, the one thing that's not true is all the stuff about hijacking the gold. I suppose it is a story about what I would have liked to do at the time and about how I think it could have been done.'

One of Crosbie's short stories inspired the film *The Chain*, which featured at the Cannes Film Festival in 2008 – an indication of much his growing body of work appealed to the outside world. His son, a filmmaker in his own right, was responsible for the production and the story mirrored real-life events. Crosbie explained at the time of the film's launch: 'As usual the story is based on someone I have known. This time it was a notorious killer who used to carry a dog chain as a weapon because he was too well known to the police to risk carrying anything else. Whenever he saw anyone that might be the police, he would simply stand holding the chain calling for a pretend dog called Rover. The story is about him when he gets older, about how he gets on with his family and about how he handles the youngsters, who love to give him a hard time about being past it.'

His work as an author and screenwriter added an air of respectability to the persona of the black sheep of the Crosbie clan. He revealed in an interview with the *Daily Record*: 'None of the rest of my family, including cousins and aunts and uncles, have ever had as much as a parking ticket, so I have been a total disgrace to the family.

'When I left school I went to the shipyards to be a welder. My father tried to stop me; he was an incredibly principled man, and he worried about where that might lead me. But I had watched my father coming in from work every night filthy and shattered, never taking a day off and I just couldn't understand it. I wanted more. I got bored quickly of the shipyards and went to join the RAF when I was 17. I thought you got to be a pilot when you joined the RAF, so when I found out that wasn't the case I left as soon as I could.'

From there he moved on to various less noble enterprises, both in London and on home soil. Once back in Glasgow, he launched a firm making gates and other ironwork, building up the business and branching out into furniture manufacturing. Crosbie added, 'The business was a great success but, in truth, I was always up to things and the reason was simply that I found it so easy to do. I should have stopped while I had the business, but I just couldn't because it was just such easy cash.'

In his seventies by the time *Ashanti Gold* hit the bookshops, Crosbie was asked whether he might revert to his old ways at some stage in the future, despite his advancing years. The reply was certain, loud and very clear: 'I just couldn't help myself, but I think I'm too old for it all now. My life is all about writing, cycling, seeing my family and going on holiday these days.'

6

The Crime that Rocked the Capital

Gone in 90 seconds – not a Hollywood blockbuster but how a chillingly executed heist from a jewellery store in the heart of Scotland's capital could be described. In that astonishingly short period of time, armed raiders succeeded in snatching more than £730,000 worth of jewellery and making their escape. They evaded capture by motorbike through Edinburgh's crowded city centre whilst shop- and office-workers thronged the streets at the end of another day's work.

For the staff at the flagship branch of Rox, the national chain of boutique jewellers, it was a harrowing experience as they came face to face with robbers whose determination matched their aggression. Those involved required counselling in the aftermath as they came to terms with the experience they had been put through.

A crisp winter's evening provided the backdrop to a piece of high drama on 15 January 2013. The post-Christmas sales were in full swing but, for the shadowy figures who approached Rox that night, the discounts were of little consequence. The clock was showing 17:13 when the doors of the shop burst open. A hooded figure led the charge, brandishing a revolver as he ran through the shop towards the stunned staff. Dressed in dark clothing and gloves, he made a beeline for the counter at the rear of the store where two members of the Rox team were stationed, aiming the handgun at their faces in a terrifying attack on innocent employees.

Sales manager Ho Suet So and sales assistant Samera Afzal were those unfortunate enough to be caught in the middle.

After being barked at with the instruction not to move, terrified Samera had the barrel of the gun thrust into her side as she was dragged across the shop to an area containing a number of particularly intricate pieces – including a £100,000 diamond collar, which appeared to be a specific target. As the gunman took control, his accomplice wasted no time in setting about his duties. Using a small axe, he systematically worked his way up the length of the showroom. First the cabinet glass was smashed and then the contents were hurriedly stuffed into a rucksack before the routine was repeated at the next cabinet. Distinctively, the axeman was left-handed. In just a minute and a half, the bag was brimming with high-value goods and the raiders were ready to make their exit, fleeing into the darkness of the night and leaving the staff cowering in the ransacked shop.

Whether the pair knew it or not, the store's manager, Katy Lawrence, had heard the drama unfold from her office and, although it was out of view, had immediately pressed a panic alarm connected to police headquarters. It was little defence against a criminal outfit clearly drilled for speed. They could have stayed for longer and ensured every last item was cleared from the cabinets but they didn't, presumably because they were conscious that an alarm was likely to be triggered. They wasted little time in simply exiting the building and getting a valuable head start on the police as they raced towards the scene. It may have lasted just 90 seconds but the incident will be a lifelong nightmare for the three women who suffered dreadful intimidation from violent armed robbers.

The event has been replayed thousands of times since it happened. The whole episode was captured by CCTV cameras trained on the shop and, unusually, the footage was made available for public consumption in the months that followed.

The headlines screamed out details of what was billed at the time as a £1-million heist. It flew in the face of the old adage that there's no such thing as bad publicity – for Rox, it was not the type of story the marketeers had in mind when they had prepared for the launch of the glitzy and glamorous Edinburgh store just a few months before the raid. The sleek store is located in the restored Assembly Rooms building on George Street, a stout presence in Edinburgh's prestigious New Town. More than two centuries old, the distinctive building has been a cultural beacon for generations in the city, playing host to such luminaries as Dickens and Thackeray down through the years.

In 2012, an 18-month refurbishment programme was completed, restoring the A-listed building to its former glory. Funded by the City of Edinburgh Council with contributions from several partners in the heritage and arts fields, the sensitive restoration included the provision of retail space within the complex and Rox was among the businesses to seize the opportunity to buy into a slice of the capital's history as was beauty brand Kiehls.

On 23 October 2012, the Glasgow-headquartered jeweller, which already had outlets on the west coast and in Aberdeen, unveiled its new Assembly Rooms base at a lavish launch party. Having invested in the region of £1 million in the outlet, the firm's managing director, Kyron Keogh, promised to provide the 'ultimate luxury shopping experience for diamond lovers and luxury watch connoisseurs'. What he could not have anticipated was the interest his new pride and joy would attract from a far less savoury section of the population – the type who came wielding an axe and revolver rather than an array of credit cards.

The terror on the night of the robbery was a far cry from the high spirits on the evening of the store's launch. More than 300 guests attended the event, with chart icon Labrinth providing the star quality and a host of well-known names from the Edinburgh scene attracted by the glitz and glamour of the occasion. With canapés provided by Jamie's Italian, a neighbour of Rox, and cocktails by Sloane's Gin, it was a party that went with a swing. The 2,500-sq.-ft shop, complete with what the company described as a 'Thrill Room' equipped with a champagne bar, represented an exciting addition to the thriving luxury goods sector in Edinburgh. Recession? What recession?

The design of the flagship Edinburgh store, by the firm Graven Images, has proved to be a winning formula and has been recreated during the firm's rapid expansion in recent years. Graven had provided the team behind the five-star Blythswood Square hotel in Glasgow and Hotel Missoni in Edinburgh and were bringing that boutique hotel feel to the world of retail through its work with Rox.

The build-up to Christmas 2013 brought a £1-million investment by the jewellery company's bosses as they moved into England for the first time. First came the opening of a store in Leeds and then an impressive outlet in Newcastle. It was the biggest store in the growing Rox chain and featured an in-house Gucci shop to set it apart from its competitors. The success in Scotland's capital had helped drive forward that recent English move. Initially employing a dozen staff, the Edinburgh boutique store opened in time to meet the anticipated Christmas rush. With a glittering array of diamond jewellery and bespoke pieces alongside watches by globally renowned brands such as Raymond Weil and Hublot, it was designed to be a destination rather than simply a shop.

A few years earlier Multrees Walk had been established just a short stroll from the Assembly Rooms – a shopping zone which became home to Harvey Nichols and Louis Vuitton amongst other famous names as the New Town went from strength to strength. The influx of top-end retailers did not go unnoticed amongst the criminal fraternity with several high-profile incidents in the years prior to the Rox raid. Fashion store G-Star Raw had £17,000 of stock stolen when thieves knocked over a bollard with a car before ram-raiding the shop and making their exit. Similarly, jewellery outlet Links of London had already been hit and, this time, a motorbike was the chosen getaway vehicle, after the windows of the store had been smashed with a sledgehammer. Iconic bag designer Mulberry was the subject of two ram raids within the space of just four months as its Edinburgh store was relieved of more than £40,000 of stock. In both of those incidents, a car had been reversed through the store window to provide swift and easy access to the displays. And both times the perpetrators made an unhindered departure from the scene leaving Mulberry to pick up the pieces – just as their counterparts at Rox were left to do more than four years later.

There had been calls to improve security at Multrees Walk but that proved a challenge on a practical level. As a public right of way, the prospect of erecting gates to block pedestrian access was considered unworkable and finding bollards able to withstand determined thieves was proving difficult. On those occasions, the hauls were less valuable than the Rox tally but they provided the warning signs for others in the same sphere to heed. Indeed, just a few months before Rox was hit, there was an incident at a neighbouring jewellers in which £27,000 of goods were taken. On that occasion the Lime Blue store, also on George Street, had been targeted by a lone raider who, at first, asked to view a selection of diamond rings – before swiping them and making his escape on foot. The difference was that the value of the Rox thefts ran into hundreds of thousands of pounds, not tens of thousands. The raiders escaped with quality as well as quantity, with a number of particularly valuable items among the treasure trove netted by the duo.

As well as the £100,000 diamond collar, they made off with engagement rings, necklaces and a collection of watches which included a distinctive £11,000 Hublot model. All in all, 77 items were taken, including 43 rings, 24 watches, 3 pairs of earrings, 3 necklaces and 4 bracelets. To date, none of those pieces has ever been recovered and the conclusion made by police was that the haul had been stolen to order rather than taken speculatively – as was observed at the time, the goods weren't the type that could be hawked around a car boot sale.

Attempting to trace the missing stock was a priority in the days following the raid but retracing the steps of the robbers was even higher on the agenda. What was known was that the pair sped away from the George Street shop on a motorbike which had been parked nearby. It was not a quiet getaway, with the duo shouting and swearing at pedestrians to 'get back' as they made their way to the black Honda 650 bike before pulling on distinctive helmets – one white, one red – and roaring off into the distance.

The use of bikes in jewellery heists had become almost commonplace in the UK in the years leading up to the Rox raid, with their nimbleness viewed as the ideal antidote to increasing city centre congestion. Just a few months prior to the Edinburgh robbery, shoppers at a London shopping centre were stunned when a gang of six armed robbers stormed the indoor mall aboard three powerful motorbikes. They smashed their way into a jewellery store and made off with Cartier, Rolex and other big-brand items before speeding out of the Brent Cross venue and through the traffic. The value of their haul was estimated to be in the region of £2 million, demonstrating, once again, the high-stakes game those involved were dealing in.

In Edinburgh, police were able to track the route taken during the getaway after the motorbike was found abandoned in a car park on Northumberland Street a short time after the incident. It lay just a few blocks north of George Street and the Rox store but far enough away to give the escaping duo breathing space. The key was left in the ignition, a sign of the haste in which it had been dumped, and a trail of evidence was discovered in the vicinity. The crash helmets, an axe used to smash the display cabinets and gloves believed to have been worn during the robbery had been dropped in the area.

As officers studied CCTV footage and interviewed witnesses, the shop remained closed for a day after the robbery to allow a thorough investigation by scenes of crime specialists. Police also stepped up patrols in the area, as much to reassure the public and traders in the area that they were serious about tracking down the offenders. A public appeal for information was made and photographs of some of the key pieces of jewellery were issued. Initial estimates suggested £1 million of stock had been lost but, as the thorough process of sifting through the debris left behind was completed, that was revised downwards to arrive at the accurate figure of £730,000.

Snippets of information began to be filtered out by the investigating team in an attempt to garner further evidence from the public. For example, it was revealed early in the probe that eyewitnesses reported one of the assailants spoke with an English accent whilst the other was said to have a local twang. It was also revealed that it was believed, after abandoning the getaway bike, the pair had continued on their path away from the scene by taxi. Police put out an urgent appeal to Edinburgh's cab drivers to report to them with any information they might have had on the movements of the two suspects.

It was a fast-moving investigation and the same could be said for the response from Rox. In addition to making £10,000 worth of repairs, within a week the firm had spent £50,000 on a new security system for the Edinburgh store, including installing a 'smoke cloud' system. When activated, the equipment is designed to release a thick fog to disorientate and deter would-be thieves. In the immediate aftermath of the Rox raid, one British company, SmokeCloak, unveiled an evolution of the system when it launched what was believed to be the world's first DNA fog fluid. The purpose of using the fluid in the cloud systems was to tag perpetrators with a unique DNA code, providing definitive forensic evidence which would be able to place them at the scene of the crime if they came into contact with the mist. The theory was that fog was a deterrent whilst the DNA was a tool for identification and prosecution – so combining both made perfect sense.

In addition to the cloud system at Rox, a permanent security guard was recruited and a new 'lock-door' policy introduced as management took a serious approach to the protection of their staff and stock. Publicity surrounding the new measures helped spread the word that the firm meant business in its battle to beat the crooks.

Just ten days after the raid had taken place, Lothian and Borders police arrested two men, both in their twenties. Days later, a third joined them in custody and, almost two months later, the operation continued with a fourth arrest, with a swift and decisive investigation. Two of those arrested during the investigation were eventually tried and jailed for their involvement. The other two walked free before the case reached court.

It was at the High Court in Glasgow that Elliot Jorgensen, 25, and Anthony Boyd, 26, entered guilty pleas in relation to the armed raid. Prosecutor Andrew Brown QC told the court that the robbery was 'carefully planned' and 'efficiently executed'. He said Jorgensen, from Salford, was involved in the raid itself with an unknown accomplice, while Boyd, an engineer from Manchester, had a central role in the 'organisation' of the robbery.

Jorgensen was the man who brandished the revolver, leaving staff 'frozen with fear' according to the prosecution. It was also Jorgensen who unwittingly provided police with the evidence which led them to close the case – his DNA was discovered on one of the recovered gloves. That was a crucial mistake made by the pair – the perpetrator's DNA profile was held on the police database due to an earlier arrest. Having been chillingly professional up to the point of their getaway, they had begun to panic in the aftermath, detectives suggested as they faced a succession of potential witnesses on the packed Edinburgh streets. They also attempted to counter a swift response from police who were quickly scrambled to the area of the robbery.

As the investigation gathered pace, officers also uncovered CCTV footage of Jorgensen being handed a large sum of cash by three men at the San Carlo restaurant in Manchester prior to his arrest. Boyd and Jorgensen each admitted a charge of assault and robbery and it emerged the latter had previously been jailed for robbery in 2007.

Detective Inspector Bobby Deas, who led the investigation, was pleased to see the two suspects brought before the court. He said: 'This was a terrifying ordeal for the staff at Rox to endure and resulted in a large quantity of valuable jewellery being stolen from the store. Officers launched a robust investigation to trace the men involved and, with the assistance and co-operation of our colleagues at Greater Manchester Police, we were able to ensure that both men were brought to justice.'

He admitted errors had been made by the pair: 'It was a

very professional job. The value of the jewellery stolen alone shows that it was professional. We can only assume that leaving behind the item of clothing was a mistake. Obviously they would not plan to leave behind any forensic evidence. It may have been due to the response from the public, as there was quite a number of people outside the store when they came out, and the police response which saw officers on the scene very quickly. Matters may have been forced on them and they made a crucial error.'

Jorgensen was jailed for 12 years while Boyd was sentenced to 10 years. In mitigation, the court was told that Jorgensen – described as 'a highly intelligent individual' – had been 'visibly shocked' on hearing what he had put the staff members through. Meanwhile, Boyd's QC claimed gangsters had preyed on his client to become involved due to his Edinburgh connections. But Lord Matthews told Jorgensen and Boyd that those who 'gamble in such high stakes' should be prepared to face tough consequences. Prosecutors also issued a confiscation order totalling £1.5 million but received just £1 from each of the offenders at that stage because neither had significant assets.

In a statement, the Crown Prosecution Services said the two accused had acted along with others as yet unknown. The CPS said Jorgensen was primarily involved as one of the two men who actually committed the robbery whilst Boyd, who has a connection with Edinburgh, was involved in planning and facilitating the robbery.

Michelle Macleod, Procurator Fiscal for the High Court in the East of Scotland, said: 'The robbery of Rox jewellers was an audacious plan to steal hundreds of thousands of pounds' worth of jewellery in broad daylight on one of Edinburgh's busiest streets. Thankfully nobody was physically injured in the robbery but being threatened with a gun and axe was a terrifying ordeal for those working in the shop and no doubt has had a lasting effect on those who witnessed the robbery. Despite their best efforts to evade capture and thanks to the thorough investigative work of police and prosecutors, two of those responsible have today been brought to justice.'

Justice may well have been done but, for the staff and owners of Rox, there was still significant unfinished business. Samera Afzal had been left unfit to return to work after the trauma of the incident and the stolen stock remained unrecovered.

DI Deas said after the sentences were passed: 'The case isn't closed. We're satisfied with this result in court but inquiries continue to recover the missing property. We're still appealing to anyone who may have information on its whereabouts to come forward.

'Our message to anyone who believes Edinburgh may be a soft target for these kind of offences has been clearly shown that this is not the case. That's not a challenge, just a statement that the full resources of Police Scotland will be brought to bear against them.'

Within days of the raid, police in Scotland had launched a nationwide dragnet, enlisting the help of forces the length and breadth of Britain. They pieced together a picture of what had taken place in the planning stages, believing reconnais- sance had been carried out well in advance in Edinburgh. They also discovered that Boyd had made arrangements for the getaway motorbike, stolen in England, to be transported from Manchester to Edinburgh in readiness. He had it dropped off on the same Edinburgh street on which his mother lived.

DI Deas said: 'It was a very challenging inquiry and we were helped by witnesses, including staff at the shop, who provided vital evidence for this case. The staff at Rox were left extremely distressed by this incident, which was horrendous for them, but they acted professionally throughout and were able to provide us with detailed information. We received excellent support and help from other police forces, particularly Greater Manchester Police, from the outset. Edinburgh is still a relatively safe city. Events of this gravity are very rare.'

And that was not an empty statement from Deas. Prior to the Rox raid, the biggest robbery in the capital was over 15 years earlier and then the cash haul was £150,000 – few and far between but enough to send shockwaves through the jewel in Scotland's crown.

The Rox heist was by far the biggest of its type but it marked the beginning of a spate of incidents in the capital in the months which followed – albeit with limited success for those behind the subsequent raids. The Beaverbrooks store at Fort Kinnaird was broken into after thieves gained entry through the roof – with a far more dramatic aerial assault following shortly after. Macintyres of Edinburgh, located on Frederick Street in the heart of the city, was targeted on by a gang with a plan likened to a scene from *Mission Impossible*. Equipped with specialist harnesses and ropes, they planned to drop in through a glass-domed section of the roof after cutting a hole to gain access. Their audacious attempt was foiled by security staff and they fled empty-handed, leaving behind some of the gear they had brought with them for the 'mission'. A jeweller's shop on the same street, Laing's, had three Rolex watches worth £50,000 stolen during the same incredible period.

Police took the opportunity to warn Edinburgh's jewellers of the risks associated with one of the high street's most glamorous trades. With security tightened and vigilance heightened, perhaps Scotland will not see their like again.

7

Auction House Hammered

The subtleties of the international commodities markets may seem a world apart from the cut and thrust of the Glasgow underworld scene but the influence of one on the other has not been lost on those tasked with picking up the pieces after a cool, calculated and lightning-fast act of daylight robbery.

As brokers on the trading floors in the world's financial centres scrambled to keep pace with demand for gold bullion when prices peaked in the summer of 2011 – rising 70 per cent in the three years up to that point – the knock-on effects began to reverberate in everyday towns and cities the length and breadth of Britain. Stores offering cash for gold popped up on every High Street and adverts were full of offers highlighting just how precious that most precious of metals had become. For those not inclined to leave the comfort of their own home, prepaid envelopes offered a swift and hassle-free route to turn unwanted jewellery into cold hard cash.

Ordinary consumers may have been the targets for the hard sell but, for the less scrupulous, the combination of high prices and a plethora of opportunities to find a willing buyer sparked a fresh interest and, according to experts in the trade, fuelled a crime wave. Never before had there been such a fervent demand – it was a modern-day gold rush and it served to attract speculators. Small-time criminals after a quick buck were one thing but the web was spun wider than that. As one Glasgow collectables specialist and dozens of innocent families discovered to their cost, high stakes led to high-risk strategies.

For auction house McTear's, the New Year of 2012 brought anything but cheer as a robber succeeded in coolly walking away with a haul of more than 300 pieces of jewellery – with the estimated value of the ill-gotten gains ranging from £400,000 to more than £2 million – all for just 25 minutes work. That is how long it took to clear out hundreds of items which had been entrusted with auctioneers ahead of a sale. The robbery sparked a major operation by Strathclyde Police as officers played catch-up in a mystifying case. The mystery did not revolve around the circumstances of the theft – every detail was captured on CCTV. Instead, the intrigue came in the days, weeks, months and years following the raid as all 300 lots of jewellery appeared to vanish into thin air. Not a single piece has ever been recovered, despite thousands of man-hours being poured into the operation. Consequently, no charges have ever been brought in relation to one of the simplest yet potentially most profitable Scottish criminal enterprises in modern times.

The episode began at 6.55 a.m. on Tuesday, 17 January 2012. That was the time on the clock when cameras captured an individual entering the McTear's premises on the south side of Glasgow. The unexpected visitor did nothing to blend into the background on a dark winter's morning – quite the opposite, in fact. Dressed in a high-visibility vest and carrying a black holdall, he looked like any other workman reporting for duty that morning in all corners of the city. But it wasn't an honest day's graft that lay ahead – his carefully planned schedule revolved around a short burst of activity. It was bold, brazen and carried out with a sense of confidence which suggested to police that they were not dealing with a first-time offender or an opportunist. This had all the hallmarks of a well-researched and -rehearsed act.

By 7.20 a.m., the 'workman' had left the building and been driven from the parking lot in a car whose driver had been patiently waiting and watching after arriving during the course of the incident. Wearing a black woollen hat throughout, offering a degree of protection against the gaze of the surveillance equipment, he carried with him his bag – by now laden with the fruits of his 25 minutes of labour. Then, in a flash, they were gone and had disappeared into the building traffic snaking its way through Govan and out of view. The car had pulled up outside the auction house, headlights blazing, just a few minutes after the individual had made his way into the building in a carefully choreographed early morning waltz.

When McTear's staff arrived for work soon after, they discovered the door left open and the alarm system deactivated. The defences of the safe had also been rendered useless. The vault was lying open and the precious sale goods gone. Among the inventory were exquisite rings, necklaces, earrings and bracelets. All were part of a catalogue which had been expected to draw admiring glances from collectors and those genuinely wrapped up in the trade but it was a far less scrupulous audience which had, in fact, been paying the closest attention.

Police were alerted and arrived on scene to be faced with a baffling scenario – one notable for its apparent simplicity rather than its complexity. The robbery had, as investigating officers admitted during the flurry of media activity in the wake of the story breaking, appeared far too easy. There was no need for force, no need for violence or any screeching tyres or dramatic chases – just in, out and away in less than half an hour.

The first stage of the investigation revolved around the access to the building. The mere mention of an auction house provokes thoughts of dusty old buildings, creaking floorboards and Dickensian-style side streets. In reality, modern life has enveloped the trade and McTear's is a shining example. Located not in the west end of Glasgow but in the grittier burgh of Govan, the firm occupies a unit within a new-build business park off the functional but unspectacular Meiklewood Road. Framed by a low, lightly coloured brick wall, the company's premises adjoin those of a property maintenance provider. The McTear's complex comprises a two-storey office block alongside an open warehouse-style space which is accessed by roller doors. From the outside, it is a clean and practical base, belying the intricate jewels and treasures it so often plays host to. Behind the scenes are the latest systems, both in terms of security and stock control, and a sense of modern efficiency which are not the usual bedfellows of one of the world's most traditional professions.

With residential properties nestled opposite the commercial premises, the target was far from isolated but that mattered little given the inconspicuous nature of the attack. In fact, even the presence of Strathclyde's finest just a stone's throw from McTear's was not a concern for the raiders. The fact a packed police vehicle repair yard is just a short drive along Meiklewood Road and a hive of activity from day to day made the robbery all the more audacious and hinted at experienced and hardened criminals rather than opportunists. It takes a brass neck to parade past one of the biggest collections of marked cars in the region, whether those are on duty or not, in a car full of stolen jewellery.

They succeeded in gaining access without any obvious sign of bludgeoning their way in. The alarm system had been deactivated and the specialists responsible for installing the high-tech system were quizzed during the course of the investigation in an attempt to discover how that electronic safety net had been seemingly sidestepped without challenge. Similarly, the safe was opened without the use of explosives or any other crude method – posing more questions than answers. Detectives described the circumstances as 'deeply suspicious' but did not elaborate with details of their theory. They tackled the case with the vigour you would expect, given the size of the haul involved and the impact the theft had on so many innocent families.

In many ways it was an unusual one for the Strathclyde force. This was a region which was no stranger to major robberies, from the post-war years onwards, bank raiders had been a curse of the city and appeared to strike with wilful abandon and frustrating frequency. In more recent times, security van heists and ram-raiding had presented a fresh challenge but, in all of those instances, there were usually first-hand accounts from those who had been directly threatened by the gangs responsible. This time, there was nothing in that respect, limiting severely any much-needed leads and information and presenting a new challenge for the detectives at the helm. Questions arising from the situation were directed at employees in the early stages of the probe, with officers admitting the possibility that the thieves had inside help could not be ruled out until every avenue had been explored. That line of questioning drew a blank as dead ends appeared at every turn. There was no flood of information forthcoming from the public either and no clues or tip-offs regarding the incident.

But there were no dead ends for the snatch team when they made their exit, pulling out of the McTear's car park and on to Meiklewood Road. From there, they had the perfect location to slip away, with easy access to the M8 and the network of feeder roads in the vicinity. The raiders could then have made their way in a plethora of directions, whether east towards Edinburgh or deeper into inner city Glasgow. After the CCTV footage captured the getaway vehicle manoeuvring away from the auction house, the trail went frustratingly cold. Strangely, no details of the getaway car were ever publicised – no registration plate was logged and nor was there any definitive suggestion on the make or model of car used.

Detectives trawled through hours of footage attempting to put flesh on the bones of the action they knew had been played out at the Govan premises but, in truth, there was little more to add. The key details were known but the identity of those responsible remained the key missing piece in the jigsaw.

Police quickly appealed for witnesses, particularly for anyone who had seen a suspicious vehicle leaving the area, and also made contact with jewellers in Glasgow and the surrounding area. The plea was simple – be alert, be vigilant and be wary of any sudden influx of stock being offered for sale. Visits were paid to key contacts in the city and favours called in, particularly among those with their ears close to the ground on the fringes of the underworld. It seemed that, if anyone knew anything, they weren't talking about it.

To help with the attempts to pinpoint the missing jewellery, detailed images of the items were released and circulated not only to those in the trade but also to the public at large. The pictures had been compiled for use in the auction catalogue – an auction which was destined never to take place after the unexpected intervention. The stunning photographs put the loss in context – the monetary value of the haul only told part of the story of the McTear's raid. From jewel-encrusted antiquities to chic modern pieces, the inventory was as rich as it was varied. With a host of distinctive designs among those lifted by the brazen thief, hopes were high that somebody somewhere would recognise them when they eventually resurfaced. The tactic was, in part, about trying to trace the collection but also, as police admitted, largely to make it more difficult for the perpetrators to profit by making a quick and unhindered sale. Any jeweller, even the less scrupulous ones, would be forced to think twice if presented with any of those pieces.

From that perspective, it must surely have been an effective plan of attack, with the story and images gaining international exposure. From newspapers to specialist blogs and jewellery industry websites, the McTear's story was the talk of the trade. There was genuine shock and outrage from those with a keen interest in the collectables sector, as well as the usual level of speculation about the detail of the crime and the eventual destination of the remarkable collection of stolen auction items. The scope and scale of the raid were highlighted in pinpoint sharp colour with that incredible collection of pictures. There were exquisite diamond and emerald rings, stunning gem-set earrings, antique pearl collectors' items, contemporary silver pieces, watches including a classic Rolex and vintage model by Tiara of Switzerland, distinctive pendants and even a rare coin. It takes more than 10 minutes to take even a cursory glance at each of the items, far longer to make a detailed assessment.

Putting a value to the collection has been a somewhat contentious exercise. The official line was that the thief escaped with items worth in the region of £400,000 – a figure calculated using the anticipated auction values of the items, taking into account the guide prices and the expert opinion garnered prior to the planned sale. But the auctions serve as a vehicle for servicing the trade, frequented not only by collectors but also by dealers and retailers seeking stock to feed their machine. They bid low with the hope of selling high, with mark-ups going as high as five times auction values. On that basis, the estimates of the total value of the haul soared as high as £2 million. Many felt somewhere in between those two extremes would be more accurate, to take into account the breadth of the variety in the assembled pieces and the unpredictability of the market.

Outside of all of those approximations is the figure the raider could have expected to net if the holdall full of goods had been quickly dispersed in criminal circles. In that case, it was claimed a £200,000 combined price tag was realistic. The seller would have been in little position to haggle and would have been looking for a quick and easy deal.

What happened to the jewellery after it left the auction house is the key to how much it was worth. A variety of options were considered by police trying to second-guess their prey. Given the lack of hard and fast lines of inquiry to pursue, there was a great deal of guesswork and intuition called into play. The first option was that it would, indeed, have been rapidly passed into the underground network. The second – and a favourite theory in many quarters – was that the boom in high street and postal precious metal buyers would have provided an instant means of turning the stolen goods into cash. A third possibility was that the items would have been effectively scrapped – stones stripped out and sold on, metals melted down and traded on the back of the high market values. It was a disturbing scenario for many families who had hoped their precious items would find loving new homes, after making the decision to put them on the market. The thought of them being scrapped must not have been palatable. The fourth theory was that the jewellery had in fact been stolen to order – most likely for distribution overseas where the chances of arousing suspicion would be slim and where it could be filtered back on to the open market to enable the maximum return on the time 'invested' by those responsible. Detective Inspector Ian Hyland admitted early in the investigation that his team had enlisted the help of international colleagues as they cast their net wide in search of a solution. Like so many lines of enquiry, that trawl overseas did not provide a notable catch.

The hunch that foreign markets may have been involved made perfect sense. Jewellery makes for the perfect smuggler's friend – unlike drugs and other contraband, there is nothing to fear from the sniffer dogs patrolling the entry points. Just like narcotics, small quantities equated to huge value and that again made it an attractive proposition for transporting. It would not have been difficult to get the McTear's haul out of the country and that remained prominent in the thoughts of the team trying to track down the missing items.

All of the possibilities were examined by police and floated as potential explanations but the only certainty is that not a single one of the 300 missing auction lots has ever been traced by the authorities. That was not for the want of trying.

Firstly, McTear's offered a £10,000 reward for anyone who could help trace the stock or those responsible for its unlawful removal. It was a significant cash incentive and considered enough to spark a reaction on the jungle drums of the Glasgow crime scene but there was nothing but deafening silence. Either that particular community had closed ranks or they had been completely bypassed by visiting criminals with a clear remit to get in, get the goods and get out.

Secondly, a flurry of police activity in Glasgow in the weeks following the raid offered the opportunity to flush out information. Although never formally linked with the McTear's raid, Strathclyde Police mounted a raid on the market at the Barras soon after the robbery and it was theorised that those arrested – on a number of charges ranging from possessing counterfeit goods to selling stolen mobile phones – may have been in a position to shed some light on the recent events in Govan when faced with an impromptu interview panel. Just as the reward failed to provide a breakthrough, the Barras clampdown was equally disappointing in its eventual outcome for those investigating the McTear's raid. It was the latest brick wall faced by officers, who at least had the consolation of making a number of arrests on matters unrelated to the big-time robbery at the auction house. It was a small crumb of comfort for an increasingly frustrated police team, operating in the full glare of a media spotlight focused on an intriguing raid.

The failed efforts to track down and reclaim the loot were even more devastating for another party in the episode – those who owned the items stolen by the well-drilled thief.

It transpired, in the weeks following the incident, that those who had entrusted their prized possessions with the auctioneer would not be entitled to any compensation for their loss. The auction lots were not covered by any form of insurance proffered by McTear's – instead, the responsibility lay with the owners rather than the keepers. Household policies, it was suggested, would come into play to offer recompense for the missing goods – but that was cold comfort to many, particularly those who did not have a valid policy covering the missing pieces.

McTear's managing director Brian Clements said at the time: 'A number of our clients lost items in the theft and we want to do everything we can to recover the jewellery and return these unique pieces to their rightful owners. We are working closely with Strathclyde Police and the independent charity Crimestoppers as the inquiry continues and we are hopeful that the reward will help to uncover some additional information that will help the authorities to identify and prosecute those involved.'

Slowly owners began to go public with their displeasure, as the realisation struck that cherished possessions had, most likely, vanished forever. It was made all the more painful by the fact that crime had been captured on film, yet there was still no real prospect of identifying or catching the perpetrator.

The proliferation of CCTV cameras in the Meiklewood Road area and the ability to post pictures of the stolen items online made the investigation a very modern affair but the crime itself was nothing new in Glasgow. As long as the city has had auction houses, it has also been home to crimes targeting those establishments. From straightforward break-ins to mysterious incidents bringing claims and counter-claims, Glasgow has seen it all.

One of the most bizarre episodes came in the summer of 1929, when the authorities were alerted to a problem at an auction house on Union Street, in the shadow of Central Station. Police arrived to find the premises had been broken into during the night, along with a neighbouring optician's, and thieves had made off with a haul of animal furs said to be worth in excess of £7,000 – a huge sum in the 1920s. According to the owner, a London fur trader by the name of Caroline Wisenthal, the collection included more than 2,000 skins in total. Everything from fox fur to the humble musquash – now more commonly known as the muskrat – was among them.

Officers sent to survey the crime scene found skeleton keys and a jemmy abandoned as though the culprits had been disturbed, as well as a selection of goods left behind despite being apparently packed to be lifted. Police considered the raid to be the work of 'experienced' thieves and said a motor car – a rarity among the criminal fraternity and certainly among 'common' thieves – had been used. That bizarre fur heist brought a disputed insurance claim, with the policy provider reluctant to pay out – so, like auction crime itself, insurance wrangles too are nothing new.

In the aftermath of the 2012 theft, McTear's spoke openly about subsequent improvements made to security – a sensible attempt to ward off any potential copycat attacks. Despite more than 170 years of experience in the trade, the company was still learning lessons in a line of business which, in many ways, has not changed since its founders first opened the doors of the auction house in central Glasgow in 1842.

William Burrell, founder of the now renowned Burrell Collection, was among the early customers found browsing for a bargain in those formative years. In more recent times, McTear's has enjoyed a resurgence, with the switch to their modern premises in Govan aiding growth and bringing the auction experience into the 21st century. Fine wines and whisky now have their own place on the annual calendar of events, attracting bidders from across the globe and earning a place among the world's best auction houses according to observers in the collectables arena. The robbery did little to tarnish a reputation established over more than a century and a half of trading – and nor did it stall the conveyor belt of interesting and enthralling items being offered for sale.

McTear's has risen to take a large share of the Scottish auction market, seizing the opportunity to expand after Christie's withdrew from the Glasgow scene. Although world-renowned names such as Christie's still dominate the sector globally, even the biggest in the business are not immune to falling victim to calculating criminals. Early in 2013 a gang of three, all based in England, were found guilty of obtaining £1-million worth of jewellery and other luxury goods from a string of auction houses – including Christie's and Bonham's. Farouk Dougui, Jabey Bathurst and Simohamed Rahmoun used a simple method to fund lavish lifestyles, quickly amassing riches during a seven-month period. The trio used credit card details stolen from overseas to register as telephone bidders for auctions containing high-value lots. Once successfully won, the items were collected before unsuspecting auction houses were aware the buyers or their means of payment were not genuine. It was described in court by prosecutors as a 'very modern way of stealing'. It was yet another thing for the auctioneers to contend with during the naturally fast-paced spirit of sale days, amid the other security concerns which fit hand in glove in an industry in which any company is only as good as the stock it sells. The better the quality and the higher the value, the greater the risk of an attack by criminals with increasing ingenuity.

Of course, the age-old means are far from extinct – regardless of improvements in surveillance technology. Scottish artist Douglas Gordon, a Turner Prize winner, discovered that to his cost late in 2012 when it was revealed that his solid gold sculpture, entitled *The Left Hand and the Right Hand Have Abandoned One Another*, vanished from Christie's storage facility in London – despite the firm's boasts of being 'the world's premier storage provider for fine art, antiques and collectibles'.

Stealth and deception had apparently been two of the traditional ingredients used for that particular crime, which was a headline grabber when it became public knowledge.

With fire-proof steel and concrete construction, as well as 24-hour security cover, Christie's premises were designed to be every thief's nightmare but, instead, it was the artist who was left gnashing his teeth. Gordon, who learned his trade as a student at the Glasgow School of Art, had traditionally stored his work at a gallery in Paris but the piece had been in London after being on show in England. At the end of that Buckinghamshire exhibition, the piece – which had been available for sale – was carefully transported to the Christie's storage facility in Westminster for what had been expected to be safe keeping. It proved to be anything but.

Gordon was stunned by the theft and angry that there had been a delay of two weeks in informing him of the incident, commenting at the time: 'Apparently an employee randomly picked up the box it was in – and discovered it was a bit light. Apart from the fact it's outrageous that something might get stolen from Christie's, I still own the work and I am creator of the work. There's something going on here about value and the way the artist is treated in all of this.'

That feeling of betrayal is common among victims in cases where thefts relate to items of sentimental value. Just as Gordon was attached to his piece through his artistic bond, so too were the families hit by the McTear's raid. In many cases they had managed to resign themselves to selling on those pieces to a good home, but it was the uncertainty of the theft and not knowing where the jewellery was destined for that nagged away at them. It could, after all, have been melted down.

Just as had been pinpointed in the McTear's raid in Glasgow, the motivation for the theft of Gordon's distinctive work was not artistic – it was, according to investigators, most likely based on global economics. With gold prices buoyant and analysts predicting a continued upward trend in the top-line figure, it was a commodity which curried favour as an investment option worldwide. That seemingly unquenchable thirst for the metal was not restricted to canny individuals. Central banks were spending billions on bullion and committing to shipments of tens of tonnes at a time – meaning the Brazilian banking community and the Barras are not so far apart after all.

8

An Ugly Secret

For thousands of visitors each year, the Pentland Hills represent an oasis of calm and tranquillity – a world away from the hustle and bustle of Edinburgh's frenetic city life, just a short drive away. Rolling hills, enchanting glens and babbling brooks paint a picture-postcard image of Scottish country life but that enticing landscape hides a grisly past.

Close to 30 years have passed but, for the families involved, the pain remains as fresh as the snowfall which blanketed the scene in January 1985. What, on first inspection, appeared to be little more than a winter road accident soon transpired to be one of the bloodiest heists ever played out on Scottish soil.

When local farmer John Graham first discovered an army Land Rover lodged in a ditch at the edge of a quiet country track, lights still glowing and window wipers on, it marked the unfolding of a nightmarish scenario for Britain's armed forces. It was a snowy winter's day, with the rural route made treacherous by the thick covering. For Graham those conditions were nothing new and didn't stop the daily routine. He was en route for a local garage to drop his car off for a service on the morning of 17 January when he spotted the stricken vehicle. He and his wife did not stop at that point but, on their return up the winding track, they took time to investigate. Spotting blood on the front seat and a shattered front window, the farmer's concern grew and he contacted police to alert them to his discovery. Unbeknown to the farmer, the police were already searching for the Land Rover after being contacted by concerned army officials on the back of a chain of events which had sparked suspicion at the nearby Glencorse Barracks.

Following a trail of blood in the snow, police officers were soon met by a gruesome discovery. For over two and three-quarter miles, they were led by the vivid red line in the snow to a perplexing crime scene. At the remote and disused Loganlea Cottage, they found three bodies – each had been shot dead. The victims were all army personnel – retired Major David Cunningham, Staff Sergeant Terrence Hosker and Private John Thomson.

The scene, on the Flotterstone Glen road and near to the Loganlea Reservoir, was sealed off and examined painstakingly by the Lothian and Borders constabulary as they set about the task of establishing the facts of a chilling crime in what traditionally had been one of the most peaceful patches of the force's sprawling beat.

Major Cunningham was found at the top of a flight of steps leading to the cottage's garden while his two colleagues were at the foot of those same stairs. Determining whether they had been killed at the scene or simply dumped there was one of the first tasks for the investigating team to establish. They also had to try to get to the root of the motive for the crime and discover who would be capable of carrying out such a horrifying attack on three servicemen.

Police photographers moved in, capturing every detail of the scene in the crucial early effort to log evidence. But it was not so much what they found at the scene which shaped the investigation but rather what was missing. The three army men had been making their way back to base with almost £20,000 – the payroll for their comrades at Glencorse. The sack stuffed full of money, freshly collected from a branch of the Royal Bank of Scotland in the town of Penicuik, was nowhere to be seen. The motive for the killings quickly became clear. With the 'why' seemingly clear, the 'where' and the 'who' were the next elements to be tackled.

Today the roadside Loganlea Cottage, once used by water workers, still stands empty, its windows neatly shuttered, and the site is enveloped by the inviting countryside it nestles within. The nearby reservoir is a popular fishing spot, a haven from Edinburgh's city trials and tribulations. The house remains a point of interest for walkers taking in the beauty and tranquillity of the Pentland Hills. Few are aware of its hidden past and that the seemingly quaint building has an integral part in Scotland's criminal history. In 1985, it was a crime scene, with police throwing resources at a type of crime which fortunately was at the time and still is today, rare. It was brutal, it was callous and it rocked the close-knit country community around the Pentlands to the core.

The fact three men had been murdered in cold blood ensured the subsequent manhunt was one of the biggest and most concerted ever mounted. The fact all three were army men intensified the shock people felt over their deaths and the services' cloak of invincibility seemed to have been thrown to one side. Tensions ran high around the forces during that era, heightened by the troubles in Northern Ireland. Indeed, the notion that the IRA could somehow have been involved bubbled beneath the surface at the earliest stage of the investigation. What army insiders described as the 'efficiency' and 'ruthless violence' of the operation bore hallmarks of an IRA ambush. The more usual modus operandi for the terrorist cells was bomb attacks, which had been a feature throughout the 1970s and 80s, but it was impossible to rule out a change of tactic as the Troubles continued and tensions remained heightened. Just a year prior to the Penicuik slayings, five people had been killed in the high-profile bombing in Brighton during the Conservative Party Conference but, in the decade prior to that, soldiers and their families had been deemed legitimate IRA targets. Twelve had been killed in 1974 when an army coach was bombed in northern England and, in 1982, eleven died when bomb attacks directed at army personnel were launched in London's Royal Parks.

Terrorism was at the forefront of everyone's mind initially but the evidence did not stack up. Scotland had publicly been declared as safe from IRA attacks and, as the circumstances were examined further, it became clear robbery, not politics, was the motive. Officers began to look at the alternatives. In the early stages every avenue was explored, with detectives not clear whether it was a lone assailant responsible for the grisly incident or a group. The prospect of an experienced group of professional thieves being on the loose was the fear held by detectives. What they were certain of was that they were dealing with a cash heist.

It transpired that the army, Britain's first line of defence, guarded the country with more diligence than they did the force's money. A familiar routine was revealed as a probe into the missing money began – with the payroll run following a tried and tested pattern. Rather than an armoured security van, as used by banks to transport cash, a canvas-roofed army Land Rover was used to make the journey from the Glencorse Barracks to Penicuik and back again. The trusty Land Rover had been part and parcel of army life since they were first developed in the late 1940s, evolving over the years but remaining true to the rugged original concept. Loved by enthusiasts – with a dedicated ex-military Land Rover association boasting a very active membership – they have served well in outposts all over the planet. From carrying supplies and troops to serving as field ambulances, their versatility has been a boon for the army for decades. But, with no security features and certainly no turn of pace to escape from a tight situation, the Land Rover was never designed to be a cash-carrying vehicle. Regularly using a standard-issue vehicle on a payroll run appeared to be remiss but that was the procedure.

It would usually be manned by three people – Major Cunningham, who was the payroll chief for the base at Glencorse, as well as a driver and an additional 'guard'. Perhaps in a nod to the lack of external security features on their vehicle, the crew was under strict orders – no stopping, no passengers, drive directly to the bank and return immediately. Those on duty were told they could be diverted from their predetermined route by police but they were still not permitted to leave the vehicle – instead, in those circumstances, they would have to follow police to the nearest station.

Unfortunately, not all of the security instructions were adhered to in the months leading up to the heist – not least on the fateful day. The crew was detailed to drive the few miles to the branch, collect the exact sum required to fulfil the varying requirements for the wage bill and return. The amount depended on how many men were to be paid and what the individual pay packets contained on any given date – anything up to £60,000 at a time. On the day in question, it was £19,000 – still a considerable haul, when you consider the average house price in Britain in 1985 was £31,000. The money was due to be paid to a batch of new recruits following their passing out parade at the base the following day, a monthly occurrence and one which was always preceded by a cash collection. It was the predictability of the cash run which made the heist feasible – but, despite the lack of traditional security measures, it would surely take a brave or foolish gang to target a group of soldiers. Perhaps that explained the deadly force used.

On Thursday, 17 January 1985, the Land Rover and its crew left Glencorse barracks just after 9 a.m. Soon after, they arrived at the Royal Bank of Scotland on John Street in Penicuik and pulled up in the car park to the rear of the building, using the back entrance leading from the car park into the heart of the branch. Located in a row of retail units, the bank's town-centre location fostered a sense of security and there was no hint of the looming danger when the large money bag was collected.

Back at the base, colleagues of the three men out on payroll duty became concerned when they did not return on schedule and notified police, prompting a search in and around Penicuik. It was at around 11 a.m. that officers were alerted to the abandoned vehicle on the track leading off the main Edinburgh to Biggar road, near the Flotterstone Inn.

Army chiefs vowed to do everything they could to aid the investigation, particularly when the intense focus began to be directed towards the organisation itself. It stood to reason, police believed, that knowledge of the payroll run and the use of a firearm pointed towards an 'inside' job. It was a sickening realisation for all connected with the regiments stationed in the region and it also sent reverberations far beyond Scotland's borders.

Soldiers stationed at Glencorse and the nearby Ritchie Camp, at Kirknewton, were interviewed on the day following the robbery – but not before the entire battalion at Ritchie had been paraded in battledress to allow their uniform to be inspected for any telltale blood stains. In that sense, the discipline at the heart of the army was a great help to detectives. There was a sense of order and protocol during those crucial early stages. They knew where everyone was and they had access to well-kept logs of people's movements and other aspects of life at the base. That gave a significant head start to those officers detailed to deal with the colleagues of the murdered soldiers. There was no time for a softly-softly approach, despite the shock and grief resonating through the troops and it was a case of getting straight to work.

Detective Inspector James Watt of Lothian and Borders Police was among those sent to Ritchie Camp. Soldiers were quizzed and records scoured for information to aid the inquiries, not least those pertaining to the weaponry held on site. Naturally those ledgers were of particular interest and within hours of arriving on base they were being carefully examined line by line.

In tandem with the work on the ground, the force was also gathering forensic and ballistic data from the scene. It was the ballistics which soon came to the fore, with specialists quickly pinpointing the type of gun used after recovering shells. It was a Sterling sub-machine gun, the type commonly used at the nearby army ranges. The model in question was capable of firing a 30-round burst in automatic mode but, crucially, could be set to fire individual shots by a marksman familiar with the gun. What the man who had fired those fatal bullets would not have bargained on was the fact that it was not only the type of gun which could be identified but the exact one. The ballistic 'fingerprint' related to tiny marks on each bullet, which experts claimed could not be replicated. Each gun left its own mark on every round it fired. Those scratches and scores are caused by imperfections in the barrel or the presence of grit or other debris. Long before forensic science became mainstream through the medium of television dramas, knowledge on the technicalities was limited.

Nine cartridges had been recovered, with analysis on those concluding that all of them had been fired by the same weapon. A meticulous log was kept of each weapon withdrawn from the armoury at the Ritchie Camp and police were quickly able to cross-reference those against the crucial 'fingerprint' left on those bullets. All of those tests were quickly conducted, with results becoming available on the evening of 18 January – the day after the payroll robbery. When those filtered through to DI Watt, he was still at the camp and in the process of interviewing soldiers.

Among them was Andrew Walker. He had first been spoken to by DI Watt at 5.30 p.m. that evening when he was questioned about his withdrawal of a sub-machine gun from the armoury the previous day. He had signed it out at around 8 a.m. on 17 January, with the apparent intention of using it for weapons training with a young soldier at Glencorse. He had backed up his story by naming the soldier he was tutoring, arousing no hint of suspicion at the time as he frequently withdrew weapons during that period and was a familiar face. He had returned it at around 2 p.m. on the same day, with no concerns raised. Although Walker had access to a gun of the type used in the robbery, he was not considered a suspect at that stage. His explanation for having the weapon was plausible and, despite some disciplinary brushes during his army career, he was considered trusted enough to have open access.

At 9.15 p.m. he was called in front of detectives to answer further questions. In a fast-moving investigation, by 10.30 p.m., Walker was again spoken to by police to be informed further information had come to light and, in the early hours of 19 January, the call came through to confirm that the gun Walker had had in his possession was the one which had fired the deadly shots. He was immediately cautioned.

Walker was 31 at the time and his address was given in court

The scene at the Securitas base in Aberdeen following the audacious raid in which the culprits exited through the front doors after abseiling through the roof. Picture courtesy of Newsline Scotland.

Above. Police study the wreckage of the burnt-out getaway cars abandoned near an Aberdeenshire church following the Securitas raid in Aberdeen. Picture courtesy of Newsline Scotland.

Left. The British Linen Bank's crest was a familiar feature on the High Street during the post-war years.

Top. The Rob Roy Road House was the staging post for the gang who pulled off the raid on the Ibrox branch of the British Linen Bank.

Above. This e-fit image was issued by police aiming to trace the gang who donned police uniform as their disguise during their attack on a cash delivery in Glasgow.

Right. A Milner safe similar to this one was overcome by the cunning group of thieves responsible for the Shettleston raid.

Above. This image is taken from the CCTV footage which captured the terrifying scene as two robbers ransacked the Rox store in Edinburgh.

Left. These were among the items stolen from Rox.

Left. Images of the haul from the attack on McTear's were quickly circulated but none of the pieces has ever been recovered.

Andrew Walker (highlighted) was a serving member of the Army when he carried out his brutal and murderous plot. Picture courtesy of *The Scotsman*.

Police are pictured at the remote Flotterstone Cottage after the discovery of the victims of the Army payroll heist. Picture courtesy of *The Scotsman*).

The Glenuig Post Office was among the rural buildings viewed as easy targets by raiders who had travelled from England.

A Vauxhall Cavalier similar to this one was used by the gang which struck at ASDA's store at The Jewel in Edinburgh.

British Linen Bank notes were eventually discovered stashed in Edinburgh after a messenger had been stabbed to death trying to protect his precious cargo.

Tweeddale Court in Edinburgh has a dark history as the scene of one of the country's most notorious crimes.

Howard Wilson is led from court after being convicted of his heinous crime. Picture courtesy of *The Herald*.

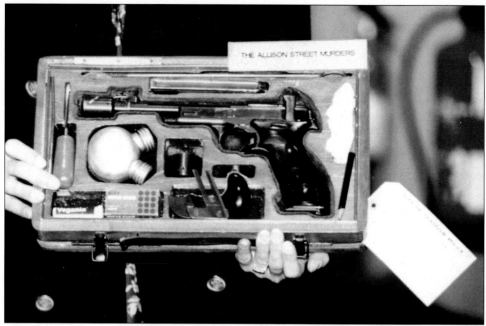

THE ALLISON STREET MURDERS

Above. The gun used by Howard Wilson. Picture courtesy of *The Herald*.

Right. The Bowers brothers were responsible for a cold and calculating series of raids on both sides of the border.

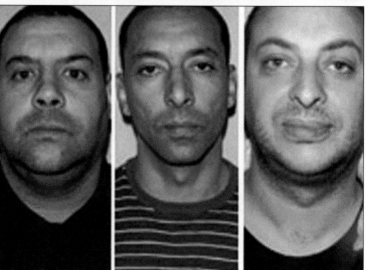

Police outside Drumlanrig Castle after one of the most precious paintings in the estate's collection had been stolen. Picture courtesy of *The Herald*.

Left. Madonna of the Yarnwinder by Leonardo da Vinci became one of the world's most wanted stolen artworks.

Above. Black rhino horns such as these are among the antiquities which are sought after by underworld figures.

Above. The Stone of Destiny in Westminster Abbey.

Right. The police carrying the Stone of Destiny away from Arbroath Abbey, April 1951.

as Kaimes Avenue, Kirknewton. He was charged with the murder of Cunningham, Hosker and Thomson. It was alleged he shot them with a sub-machine gun and robbed them of £19,000 between the Royal Bank of Scotland and Flotterstone. He denied all charges, lodging a special defence of alibi.

At his High Court trial in Edinburgh, staged over the course of three weeks in May 1985, evidence from 125 witnesses was given and it painted a picture of desperate actions by a desperate man.

Walker was due to depart with the 1st Battalion the Royal Scots for a tour of duty in West Germany, leaving behind his wife and two young children. Before then, he had debts to settle, including more than £1,000 of finance on a car, an Alfa Romeo, repayments for which had ground to a halt, and other outstanding balances. It transpired that he had hitched a lift in the payroll Land Rover in November and December 1984, testing his ability to breach security procedures. On each occasion, he had done so simply – first thumbing a lift back to base and then secondly managing to blag a seat in the vehicle for a run to Penicuik by claiming he needed to visit the bank's cashpoint. That had given him the confidence to follow through with his plan to hijack the 4x4. The problem was – and Walker was well aware of it – that, by using his uniform to gain a seat on the return journey from the bank on that January morning, he would be easily identifiable to his colleagues which meant the only way of escaping with the money was for him to kill those men.

It has always been assumed that, after persuading the crew to give him a lift back to base, he chose an opportune moment during the journey to produce the sub-machine gun he had concealed within his uniform. A witness reported hearing a shot near to the Mauricewood housing estate, on the approach to Flotterstone. And it is believed Major Cunningham may have been the first victim at that point. Hosker is thought to have been the next to suffer, with Thomson, the driver, spared only until they had reached their destination at Loganlea Cottage. Where the plan began to unravel was as Walker made his escape in the Land Rover. Fresh snowfall and ice on the track, coupled with his hasty retreat, led to the jeep to careering off course and into a ditch. From there, his plan for an exit on four wheels was replaced by one on two feet.

Walker is known to have hitched a lift, first in the direction of Edinburgh and then back towards Penicuik, where he retrieved a distinctive Fiat Mirafiori. He had borrowed the car from a fellow soldier, spinning a yarn to explain away his need for the vehicle. The reason he really required the car was to help him to establish an alibi. First he drove into Edinburgh and refuelled at a petrol station in Liberton, making a deliberate scene when he was a penny short of the £5.01 total to ensure he stuck in the mind of the attendant. He then went to pay a visit to a former girlfriend in another part of his plan to build an alibi for the morning in question. He then returned home, dropping off the borrowed car and handing the gun back to the armoury. He handed over £100 to his wife, despite having had to borrow £5 from her earlier that day. He explained away the windfall by saying he had found a bag of money hidden beneath a wall whilst out jogging that morning. He also went ahead and ordered an £8,000 Austin Maestro laden with extras, for which he had promised to pay cash. The car was left-hand drive, equipped for the time he was due to spend on duty in Germany, and the order clearly demonstrated he was confident that he would soon be en route for his continental destination, unhindered by the investigation into the triple murder of his colleagues.

Whilst he appeared unperturbed, the incident was the talk of the army community – not surprisingly. Once word of the robbery began to spread, Walker even told his wife that he had been responsible – before laughing his claim off, apparently panicking after watching her break down. While he protested his innocence at home, the soldier's alibi quickly fell to pieces in a more public arena as the investigation gathered pace. Witnesses in Edinburgh placed him at the filling station an hour later than he had claimed whilst his former girlfriend, it was discovered, had not been in the city for three months at that point. The soldier's claims about his movements on the day of the crime were being picked apart piece by piece.

Another strand of the defence – his claim that he had left the gun at the barracks while he was away – was ripped apart by a twist of fortune. Whilst Walker was absent from his post as he set about putting his murderous plan into action, a search at the base had been called due to a missing Dictaphone. No trace of the Dictaphone was found but, similarly, no trace of a gun was discovered either. The weapon was quite categorically not on the army site at the time of the killings.

During the trial a picture of Walker began to emerge. It was revealed that he was known by his army colleagues as Billy Liar – a nod to his tall stories and boasts. Beneath that was a steely aggression, something he had demonstrated from a young age by reaching the semi-finals of the national amateur boxing championships whilst representing his Edinburgh club Sparta. The same fighting spirit had translated into what, at one stage, appeared to be a promising career representing Queen and country.

However, in the build-up to the murderous heist, he had fallen foul of army superiors – fined first for failing to return to his unit after leave and then again for failing to appear for duty and lying to his commanding officer. Eventually, just a week before the robbery, he was dismissed from his job as a firearms instructor at Glencorse and was returned to his battalion at Ritchie Camp.

In the words of his military record, Walker had become 'quite unreliable and was losing the confidence of his comrades and superiors'. In hindsight, that assessment was an incredible understatement of the character of a man under investigation for one of the greatest crimes in modern-day Scottish military history.

Despite Walker's protestations of innocence, a jury of nine women and six men took just 90 minutes to reach their verdict when his case went to trial – guilty as charged. The disgraced soldier was sentenced to 30 years in jail, with Lord Grieve commenting: 'You have been found guilty of what can only be described as brutal, callous and calculated murders which must bring revulsion to the hearts of all decent-thinking people. You have shown yourself to be wholly unworthy to be a member of a famous and distinguished regiment. Your conduct has been quite inexcusable.'

Prior to the verdict being returned, Walker's defence QC had told the jury that 'being a liar, adulterer and a bad soldier on occasion' did not make him 'a callous, brutal murderer'. Those pleas were ignored by the men and women given the task of considering the harrowing evidence presented to them. The sentence equalled the longest passed in a Scottish murder case after judges were given the power in 1965 to set a minimum number of years for a life sentence. It reflected the abhorrent circumstances and went a small way towards giving the grieving families some form of closure.

In the aftermath, army officials were defiant – insisting no changes would be made to security arrangements. An army spokesman said the money carried by the payroll vehicles would not normally be enough to tempt criminal gangs to attempt a copycat efforts. However, it was revealed that Securicor had been enlisted to carry out the Glencorse run – although the military chiefs were at pains to stress that was a choice made to prevent local residents having to see the Land Rover plying its familiar route and bringing back painful memories. Despite the resounding verdict in the case, Walker lodged his first appeal within weeks of his conviction. He maintained in court that he believed the IRA had carried out the killings.

He was sent to Peterhead prison, later having his sentence increased after playing a part in a major riot at the north-east jail. He was said to have revelled in his status as one of the country's most notorious criminals although, in time, that status faded and so too did his resilience. In 2002, Walker succeeded in having his sentence reduced by three years and, in 2011, he was reported to have been transferred from Shotts Prison, where he had been moved to after his stint in Peterhead, to a private room in a Lanarkshire hospital after suffering a stroke – throwing the horrifying detail of the 1985 back into the public eye for a new generation to make their judgement.

At the time the story first unfolded, the publicity surrounding the case was huge. That attracted a new breed to the Pentland Hills – bounty hunters. The £19,000 stolen during the heist was never recovered and Walker, maintaining his innocence throughout, never revealed what had happened to it. The police theory was that the haul would have been stashed somewhere easily accessible in the aftermath of the robbery, most likely in the vicinity of the Ritchie Camp at Kirknewton where Walker had been transferred to from Glencorse shortly before the ill-fated heist. He was also known to have spent an hour in Edinburgh following the murders so it was possible it had been deposited in a bank or building society account – although no institution ever came forward to report taking receipt of the cash when the figure involved was making big headlines. Police believed they would have been made aware if that had been the case, leading them to assume the cash sat hidden somewhere in the immediate aftermath. The other possibility put forward at the time, although not by the police who had studied the case in such detail, was that an accomplice had assisted Walker and had helped ensure the money was spirited away. Investigating officers were adamant that it was a one-man operation.

The theory which many members of the public grabbed hold of was that Walker had buried his loot near to the scene of the murders, in the foothills of the Pentlands. That prospect brought a steady stream of unfamiliar visitors to the area, all seeking the £19,000 which they believed lay undiscovered in the region.

Police dismissed that idea, claiming the murderer would not have risked spending time in the area in the aftermath of the shootings and, instead, would have made a quick getaway. They carried out their own searches, including dragging water near the scene of the robbery, but turned up not a single note of the missing haul. It remains one of the few remaining mysteries yet to be solved, almost three decades on from one of Scotland's most shocking criminal episodes.

9

Scotland's Unwelcome Tourists

In the dead of night on a remote Highland rail track, a new breed of criminal discovered that Scottish law enforcement is far from toothless. With only the glow of the moon and the glint of flashlights to lift the darkness, the well-honed tracking skills of Northern Constabulary's police dogs came up trumps as a cross-border raider was brought to justice.

It was in October 2007 that convict John Hind's busman's holiday was brought to an unexpected end. The 54-year-old, from Colne in Lancashire, had set out that evening to raid a rural post office – reassured by its far-flung location and encouraging isolation. What the English visitor did not realise was that his every move was being watched by a surveillance team from the local police force. When it did eventually dawn on him that his nocturnal expedition was about to be cut short by the boys in blue, Hind headed for the hills. His escape route took him over rugged terrain as he attempted to shake off the attention of the pursuing officers but, again, the criminal had underestimated his adversaries. When the police dogs were unleashed to track their target, it was game over and brought a mini-crimewave to an end. It also represented a significant achievement for Northern Constabulary, the proud Highlands police force which was consigned to the history books when Police Scotland was introduced as part of a huge streamlining project in 2013.

What Northern Constabulary succeeded in doing during its lifespan was bringing law and order to a patch equivalent in size to Belgium. From the city streets of Inverness to the sprawling expanses of the mainland countryside and from the trunk roads of the central Highlands to the backwaters of the islands, they had it covered.

Hind was later jailed for that evening's robbery but the conviction represents just the tip of the iceberg for Scottish officers fighting a wave of English criminals sweeping into the country to take advantage of what are perceived as easy targets. And perception is a major factor in fuelling the problem. According to those involved in stemming the tide, there is a growing consensus of opinion among the criminal fraternity south of the border that Scotland is somehow trailing behind their own land when it comes to crime prevention and detection. As a result, all roads lead north for the gangs intent on seeking out fresh hunting grounds and travelling north in numbers to carry out raids on what they view as soft touches in the isolated corners of a country more renowned for its rolling glens and tranquil lochs than organised crime. But those same gangs have been given a stark warning – there is no place to run and no place to hide. With individuals and gangs responsible for crime tours under lock and key after successful prosecutions in the Scottish courts, detectives have vowed to continue their efforts to ward off the threat posed by touring villains they believe are responsible for a series of unsolved robberies that follow a similar pattern to closed cases in recent years.

As Aberdeen-based Detective Inspector David Hadden warned, officers were braced for the challenge posed by the alarming trend. He said, 'Criminals from other parts of the UK intent on travelling to the area to commit crime should be aware they will be met with a hostile reception and will be vigorously pursued.' DI Hadden had played his part in high-profile investigations into the modern phenomenon, not least the conviction of a trio of Liverpudlians for a botched attempt at robbing a north-east bank in what was described as an 'organised' operation by a visiting group of 'villains' by a High Court judge during a prominent trial. And, indeed, they did find a hostile reception from Hadden and his colleagues. Although, admittedly, that did not serve as an absolute deterrent.

In 2013, the Grampian region found itself in a whirlwind of activity. More than half a dozen cash machines in and around Aberdeen were allegedly targeted and a string of golf centres raided as high-value goods vanished into the night. Paul Lawrie, golf's 1999 Open champion, was among those on the receiving end when £30,000 worth of clothing and equipment went missing from his Deeside driving range and golf course. Lawrie, using his public profile to vent his anger, did not hold back, describing those responsible as 'scumbags' in a volley delivered through the medium of Twitter.

What followed the proliferation of thefts and attempts was a very high-profile game of cat and mouse that ended when a stolen Audi, bearing false registration plates, was recovered in woodland in Aberdeenshire and subsequently an arrest was made. At the time of writing, the man in question, a Liverpudlian, is awaiting trial in connection with a number of alleged incidents.

Those involved in the operation vowed to leave no stone unturned, something officers covering the more rural beats continue to pride themselves on. The promise of vigorous pursuit was best demonstrated in the Highlands during the apprehension of Hind and some fellow Englishmen suspected of a series of Post Office raids at remote locations dotted across the north of the country.

During the course of the summer and autumn of 2007, a total of £45,000 in goods and cash was taken during incidents at a string of locations in Moray and the Highlands. As the investigation progressed, detectives came to the understandable conclusion that the raids were linked and went public with their theory that the perpetrators were not local. It had the hallmarks of a well-organised and calculated campaign of thefts, rather than spur-of-the-moment or opportunistic attacks.

While Hind and Matthew Peters from Bournemouth were found guilty of stealing a safe from Glenuig Post Office – the incident in which Hind was arrested under the cover of darkness after being tracked by the police dogs – the pair had already been formally acquitted after being charged with carrying out 13 other break-ins at post offices and commercial premises in the Highlands during the same period. Hind and Peters were also acquitted of stealing a car in the village of Lochailort and using it to assault a Fort William-based police officer to the danger of his life. Peters, however, was found guilty of stealing a safe during a break-in at Embo in Sutherland. On that occasion, the accused, who was 40 at the time, escaped with £7,000 in cash and stock worth £1,926. No value for the Glenuig raid was ever disclosed.

The convictions for the Glenuig and Embo thefts brought to an end one of the longest-running legal sagas the Highlands have ever witnessed. The decision of the jury at Wick Sherriff Court came in September 2011 – almost four years after the duo had been apprehended by police in Glenuig. It also came after a five-week trial, a duration which set a new record for that particular courthouse. In contrast to the trial length, it took the jury just an hour to reach majority verdicts and pass a guilty verdict on each of the accused. For the normally sleepy Caithness town, that five-week period provided an injection of drama and intrigue as the details of a concerted police operation were played out in great detail. That operation had been set up to try to solve break-ins across Caithness, Sutherland, Ross-shire, Lochaber and Moray. In the end, only Glenuig and Embo were resolved – with the other 13 investigations not yet resulting in a conviction. The spate of attacks on premises in such unlikely crime scenes was headline news, as was the trial of Hind and Peters in Wick.

Like any area, Caithness suffers from occasional incidents of crime but, by and large, it is a safe and peaceful part of the country to live in. The nearest city to Wick is Inverness – a 200-mile round trip that takes more than four hours. Because of that isolation there is a real sense of community throughout the area and people look out for each other. People also have a loyalty towards the local businesses that serve the towns and villages so well – any attack on those businesses feels like an attack on the community as a whole.

There was real concern when a sudden rush of break-ins in the north and west Highlands commenced in the summer of 2007. Police made repeated appeals for information and found a willingness among the locals to help, with many people coming forward to offer assistance as the investigations progressed. It soon became apparent that officers were following a positive line of enquiry but what people did not realise until the trial of John Hind and Matthew Peters was some of the fine detail of the work being done behind the scenes.

The trial understandably drew a lot of attention. It was the talk of the town for weeks on end. Because of the rarity of that type of crime in the Highlands, there was a lot of media attention and the fact it involved two individuals who had travelled the length of the country to commit their crimes made it all the more fascinating for those following the court proceedings. It brought a realisation that no area is immune to criminality. In the aftermath, there was definitely a sense that greater attention was being paid to security and I would say that remains the case. Distance is no barrier – if somebody is determined to carry out a break-in, spending a few hours on the road to do that is not really any deterrent.

For many people, particularly those outside Scotland, there is a perception that the Highlands are some sort of untouched wilderness. There's an impression that somehow that part of the world is removed from the normal reach of the law. Obviously, that is very far from the true picture but, unfortunately, not everyone is smart enough to realise that.

The details played out in court showed the lengths Northern Constabulary went to in order to apprehend the suspects. They combined good old-fashioned police and detective work with the use of new technology as well as the skills of their police dogs to bring it to a conclusion. If that hadn't happened, there could well have been other incidents.

The reference to technology relates to the tracking of mobile phone communications which was revealed by police witnesses during the trial. Northern Constabulary statistician Maria Wright had been tasked with tracing calls from mobile phones believed to belong to Hind and Peters, using information obtained from masts throughout the area, in a bid to paint a picture of their movements. The defence solicitor dismissed Wright's evidence as 'meaningless', claiming there was no hard evidence linking the accused pair to the phones recovered by police. In addition to the mobile phone observations, it was also revealed in court that a white Vauxhall Omega – a powerful model so often the preserve of traffic police patrols the length and breadth of Britain – being used by the two men in the dock had been secretly tracked by officers who had singled the duo out as suspects following the break-ins across the north.

Detective Callum Macleod was part of a team who had been detailed to follow the pair and was on their tail on the night they chose to target the post office branch at Glenuig, a hamlet around 30 miles west of Fort William on the rugged Lochaber coast. Standing at the scene of the crime, it is not difficult to imagine why the location proved attractive to visiting criminals. The post office sits on the main road to Fort William, the A861. The geography of the branch and the fact it was targeted were surely not coincidental – with the Northern Constabulary base at Fort William a 35-mile journey away along winding country roads, a trip that would take you or me close to an hour to complete. Admittedly, officers responding to a 999 call would be able to cover the ground slightly more quickly but it was certainly remote enough to give raiders a significant window of opportunity to execute their plan and make their escape.

Location was not the only influencing factor – the fabric of the Glenuig outpost was likely to have been an attraction to John Hind as he plotted to get rich quick. The tiny green pre-fabricated building nestles in a recess carved into a hillside strewn with stones and shrubs. It sits opposite rolling fields, with a glimpse of the open waters off the coast in the distance. The building, with the simple word 'SHOP' stencilled upon its exterior and only a small 'Post Office' sign to give away its dual role, looks as though it could be prised open using little more than a tin opener. Compact and bijou, up until 2007 it had been nothing more than a simple part of the fixtures and fittings of the area but it was soon to take centre stage, as police closed in on Hind and Peters.

During the subsequent trial, DS MacLeod spoke of his team's efforts to follow the targets. A number of officers were involved on the night in question and, as the Englishmen carried out their planned raid and made off with the safe and its contents, the police team moved in. The two made their getaway along a neighbouring railway line. PC Sean McNeil was part of the chasing pack, calling after the suspects and shining his torch in their direction. He recalls, 'For a split second, they were like rabbits in headlights. They were taken a bit by surprise.'

It was left to a police dog handler to take up the chase, catching and detaining Hind in handcuffs after a difficult search in which the night's other offender made his exit. Another police dog handler and his canine sidekick had more joy in locating a safe from one of the north break-ins.

Whilst Hind and Peters were found guilty of the raid at Glenuig on the west coast, it was Peters who took the punishment at the same trial for a similar break-in on the east coast of the Highlands at Embo. The tiny Dornoch village, more than 45 miles from police headquarters in Inverness and over an hour's drive from the city, is a peaceful seaside retreat. Its post office, like the one at Glenuig, comprises a counter within a store – in this case, a newsagent's shop in a small detached building situated in a narrow lane leading down to the shore and surrounded by residential properties. Its position was clearly appealing to Peters, who was around 650 miles from his home on the south coast of England when he made off with his £9,000 haul without being apprehended but brought to justice months later during his trial in Wick. Peters was sentenced to two years in prison while Hind was hit with a 15-month jail term. However, those punishments pale into insignificance in comparison to the sentences meted out to another clutch of Englishmen found guilty of misdemeanours north of Hadrian's Wall.

Liverpool trio Anthony Jackson, Peter Purcell and Terrance Jackson were jailed for a combined period of more than 20 years in 2010, after being found guilty by a jury of an attempted robbery at an Aberdeen bank in September 2009. The travelling group were lambasted by Lord Uist as he passed down the sentences, hoping to send out a message to others intent on seeking out Scottish targets. He declared at the High Court in Aberdeen: 'Serious crimes of this sort simply cannot be tolerated and villains such as you three must expect strong sentences – not just to punish you but to deter others who may be tempted to carry out this sort of crime. It is clear that you are all Liverpool criminals who thought you could get away with this crime in Aberdeen.'

What Jackson, Purcell and Jackson thought and what proved to be the case were two very different things. They failed to evade police – having first failed to get their hands on the cash they had planned to grab during their attempted bank raid.

The drama unfolded during an eventful day on the south side of Aberdeen, with two separate incidents to keep Grampian Police on their toes. The locations were within two industrial areas of Europe's oil capital – Altens and East Tullos. Both sprawling districts are home to a mix of industrial, commercial and office premises. Major multinational oil corporations such as Shell sit side by side with car showrooms, scrap yards and small-scale enterprises scattered throughout a maze of streets and lanes criss-crossing between units of varying sizes. Those roads are busy throughout the day as one of the city's key business areas throngs with activity. The Altens and East Tullos industrial parks straddle the A90 Aberdeen–Dundee road to the south of River Dee, acting as the boundary to the city centre. It was on 11 September 2009 that the two normally unremarkable areas became the settings for some remarkable events.

Firstly, a Royal Mail van was targeted as its elderly driver went about his daily rounds. Anthony Jackson would later be convicted of the crime, striking as driver John Sim, who was in his 70s at the time, stood at a post box 30 feet from his parked works vehicle on Wellington Road. Jackson drove off with the van and its contents, as a panicking Sim was left to flag down a passing police car for assistance. The distinctive Royal Mail van was spotted in the area, drawing the attention of motorists because its doors were swinging open as it threaded its way clear of the crime scene. Fitted with an electronic tracking device, the van was later recovered after being abandoned in the Altens industrial estate. A resident of Blairs, a village in neighbouring Aberdeenshire, told the court that she had discovered a pile of burning mail, later identified as being linked to the van theft, that same evening. It was a terrifying experience for Sim, who had retired from his Royal Mail role by the time Anthony Jackson stood trial. But the event proved to be a precursor for an even more intense operation by the Liverpudlian threesome hours later.

In nearby East Tullos, a security van team was subjected to a terrifying experience as they arrived at the Halifax Bank of Scotland branch on Greenwell Road. The modern bank sits alone on a patch of ground at the entrance to the industrial estate, a small building but one which welcomes a steady stream of customers throughout the day. Its location opposite the city's Porsche and Range Rover dealerships belies its earthy, industrial surroundings. With its relatively open aspect, it was viewed as a viable target by the Liverpool gang. Equally important was its location. Just a stone's throw from Wellington Road, one of the city's main thoroughfares, it ensured an easy escape. Stretching from the fringes of the city centre to the southern suburbs of Aberdeen, Wellington Road can be a traffic hotspot but, at the time of the bank raid, around 9.30 p.m., it would have been relatively deserted – a quick and easy to navigate exit route.

The trio wore masks and dark clothing when they ambushed Christopher South and his colleague Craig Richards, brandishing metal bars as the guards visited the branch to collect money from the safe. It was every security man's worst nightmare, as the scenario they are trained for was played out – a scenario they hope never turns into reality. That night it did. South appeared as a witness at the trial of the group and told the court that he had heard rustling from bushes as he went about his duties and then had seen 'three or four' men rushing towards him. The assailants shouted and swore at their victim, ordering him to drop the cash box he was carrying before pushing him to the ground and striking him with a metal bar as he struggled to open the box. It was only then that the raiders discovered the box South was carrying was empty – a crushing blow to their get-rich-quick scheme. Compelled to rapidly change tactics, they tried to force their way into the bank in a desperate attempt to come up with a plan B but Richards had remained inside and was able to secure the building and activate his panic alarm to scramble the emergency services. One of the raiders was said by Richards to look 'a bit lost' when he refused to allow them to enter the bank. They hadn't bargained on the resilience of their victims or their admirable dedication to their role in protecting the bank's cash.

It transpired, during the trial, that the East Tullos branch had held concerns for the security van team, with Richards admitting in court that he worried about the lack of light due to overhanging branches and trees which sheltered the site from the streetlights on surrounding roads. It would appear he was not alone in recognising the potential threats to the protection of cash deliveries to the branch, with the gang clearly identifying the possibility of planning a raid.

Those responsible for the bungled attempted robbery fled the scene in a black Mazda 3 – empty-handed. The car was found two days later at the nearby Thistle Hotel in Altens.

Detectives poured hundreds of man-hours into tracing those responsible. In a high-profile trial at the High Court in Aberdeen, the perpetrators Jackson, Purcell and Jackson were all found guilty of attempted robbery at the HBOS branch. Anthony Jackson, who was sentenced to nine years in prison, was also found guilty of stealing the Royal Mail van and its contents. Purcell, who was sentenced to six years in custody, was found guilty of stealing a car, which was used in the attempted robbery, from Wellheads Industrial Estate, Aberdeen, on 10 or 11 September. Terrance Jackson, who was also found guilty of giving false details to police, was sentenced to seven years and six months in jail. All three had denied all of the charges against them. Anthony Jackson was found guilty of the attempted bank robbery by a majority jury verdict whilst the 12-strong jury reached a unanimous guilty verdict on all of the other charges. It took them just four hours to reach their verdict.

Before sentencing, the court was told all three men had a string of previous offences. Lord Uist observed: 'This was an organised crime that must have involved some degree of reconnaissance to find out what time the van would arrive at the bank. That you did not obtain any money was just down to the fact that you swooped when the guard was carrying an empty container.'

Of equal concern to the authorities was the trauma the innocent victims were subjected to during the course of a day of crime. Detective Inspector David Hadden led the investigation and said it was purely 'down to luck' that no one was seriously injured. DI Hadden added, 'These were serious crimes where members of the public legitimately going about their daily business were the victims.'

Both Anthony Jackson and Terrance Jackson lodged appeals against their conviction but both failed. The fact they and Purcell ended up behind bars represented success for Grampian Police in the fight against visiting criminals but, with one battle won, it represents just part of the war on this new type of threat.

Aberdeen in particular is no stranger to cleaning up the mess left behind by outsiders, with Midlands drugs gangs and others from Liverpool and the North-west of England on the receiving end of some aggressive detective work by Grampian's finest – leading to a string of convictions after a wave of proactive operations to curb the threat.

With a motley crew of English interlopers dealt with through the courts in the north and north-east of the country on the back of a series of raids and attempted robberies, police chiefs remain intent on sending the unwanted tourists homeward to think again.

10

A Jewel Heist with a Difference

The 1990s was the decade which brought us the Britpop movement, the advent of the internet and the cinematic explosion of *Trainspotting*. In amongst those cultural markers was another 90s phenomenon – the ram raid. Yes, it had been done before – very few criminal enterprises are entirely original, after all – but what the dawn of that particular decade heralded was a craze in the underworld which swept the country in a way which nobody could have predicted.

High-value goods were the prime targets, with electrical retailers and designer outlets the destinations of choice for those armed with a stolen car and a complete disregard for the law. The template was simple – smash your way in, clear out as much stock as possible and make your escape. In theory, the only danger was to those in the offending car but all of that changed in the late 1990s with a potentially deadly attack in an Edinburgh suburb which saw a horrifying hybrid come to the fore. It was the armed ram raid, something never before seen in Scotland and one which almost ended in catastrophe.

On 9 October 1997, two members of the security staff at the Asda superstore at The Jewel in the capital were patrolling the shop floor when they were faced with a traumatic and rapidly unfolding drama. It was early morning and the store was being prepared to open for another day's trading when the calm of the moment was broken by the sound of shattering glass and the roar of an engine as a stolen car came careering through a fire escape at speed and hurtled into the body of the supermarket. The two employees were inches from being struck as they dashed for cover but their ordeal did not end there. Two men leapt from the vehicle, one armed with a handgun, and ordered staff to lie on the floor. They proceeded to use force to get their hands on £150,000 in cash, stored in bags, which was loaded into their damaged vehicle and driven out of the crumpled emergency exit and away. Throughout the robbery, the two ringleaders had kept their faces covered by masks, giving away little in the way of clues.

The episode sent shock waves through the local community and across Edinburgh. Newspaper, radio and television reports broke the news to residents who had initially been unaware of what had caused the commotion at the store and, in the aftermath, the place became a hive of activity with a visible police presence. A trip to the supermarket is one of the most ordinary activities in day-to-day life but, all of a sudden, for the customers at The Jewel, it took on an eerie feeling as they came to terms with what had been played out at 'their' store. It may be Scotland's capital but, mercifully, its experience of serious crime has been infrequent.

The raid remained the largest robbery in Edinburgh for well over a decade, not surpassed until the £1-million jewellery heist at the Rox store in 2013. What is all the more remarkable is the fact that the bounty could have been even greater had it not been for a twist of fate which not even the most organised of raiders could have bargained for.

One of the cash dispensers at the supermarket had broken on the day of the raid, leading to a planned cash delivery of £350,000 being cancelled. Had it gone ahead as planned, there would have been £500,000 in cash within the store rather than the £150,000 which had been snatched. It was still a significant haul but, in the words of police, the situation could have been far more serious if a greater sum had been stolen and if injuries or worse had been inflicted in the process.

Terrified staff quickly sounded the alarm and police dashed to the scene from a variety of surrounding stations, including those at Brunstane and Niddrie. By the time they arrived, the thieves had vanished and officers were left to try and pick up a trail which had already gone cold. Senior detectives were enlisted and a troop of uniformed staff deployed to conduct interviews and amass evidence from the superstore.

What the boys in blue were presented with was a crime scene like few others. Far from hidden away, it was an incident in the biggest and busiest Asda store in Scotland's capital city. Inconspicuous it wasn't but potentially lucrative it certainly was. Remember, this was 1997 – cash was still king in the world of retail. Debit cards may have been introduced in the 1980s but, by the time of the heist at The Jewel, it was still true to say that half of British adults did not have one in their possession and an even smaller proportion used those cards regularly. In fact, it was not until 2004 that card spending in the UK exceeded cash transactions for the first time. Instead, ready money was the order of the day as the tills rang out in the supermarket world and feeding demand was the ever-busy network of cash machines. The Edinburgh raiders knew their target and it was not the checkouts or the store's vault they would be aiming – it was the area used to service the ATMs.

As regular as clockwork, those machines were loaded with money in preparation for the store opening its doors and the routine offered a window of opportunity to those with dubious motives. What they had to do was strike at the right time and find a way of doing that in the quickest and most effective manner. Ram-raiding provided the solution to that particular problem. They could also be assured that the fire doors would be shifted easily enough, given they could not be heavily reinforced – just the simple locking mechanism that could be pushed open from inside and forced open from the outside.

The motive was clear, the method instantly apparent and witnesses were on hand to brief the first officers on the scene. The first significant leap forward in the investigation came within hours as the vehicle used to ram through the doors of the building was discovered abandoned in a quiet residential street just a short distance from the scene of the robbery. Newcraighall Drive in Musselburgh has rarely hit the headlines, but that autumn it became the focus of intense police

activity as the Lothian and Borders force descended on the
leafy suburban track to retrieve the car, examine the area in
which it was discovered and comb the surrounding ground
for clues. Residents were identified in an attempt to pin down
evidence and gain a picture of which path the getaway route
had taken the raiders next. Few had seen anything out of the
ordinary, with the cool and composed exit at odds with the
chaos which had been left behind at the store.

Their journey from the shop to the point where they abandoned the damaged car was just over a mile. They drove out
of the Asda car park on to Newcraighall Road before joining the A1 and then quickly darting off the main road into
Newcraighall Drive. With its warren of lanes between houses
and a network of car parks peppered along its length, the street
offered plenty of spots for an undisturbed switch of vehicle.
And that was where the maroon-coloured Vauxhall Cavalier,
bearing false number plates, was discovered. It had been stolen
days earlier in Edinburgh, liberated from McLaren Road – an
upmarket residential street in the Newington district of the city.
More important than the impressive houses lining McLaren
Road was its location – just a short hop from The Jewel. Yet,
in between the car being stolen and being put to use in the
Asda raid, it must have been stored elsewhere and had the fake
plates fitted.

The car of choice was fit for purpose. Big enough and heavy
enough to smash its way into the store, fast enough to inspire
confidence in a successful getaway – but perhaps most importantly of all, it was unremarkable enough to ensure it didn't
arouse suspicion at any stage in the build-up to the main event.
Wherever it had been, it had not come to the attention of the
authorities.

The car was very much a star as far as evidence was concerned but, whilst specialists combed the Vauxhall for scientific
clues to the identity of its most recent occupants, there was
a more basic approach being taken by their colleagues. The
store's own CCTV system was a valuable source of information. Asda, as a company, has always taken store security

seriously and invested heavily in technology – not only for the safety of its staff but also to protect stock and to guard against shoplifting. By the 1990s, the systems were improving – Britain's first CCTV had appeared on the scene in the 1950s but it was not until the new millennium loomed that cameras in commercial premises became commonplace. Since 1997, the major retailers have become even more ingenious. In 2003, a system was trialled by Tesco in which individual items known to be popular with shoplifters were tagged and, when moved, they would activate a camera to hone in on the person responsible. It was a fast and effective way to monitor specific items of interest.

At The Jewel, a more basic network of cameras was in place, in keeping with the period in time, and trawling through hours of CCTV footage was a laborious process for the investigating team. It did, however, throw up new clues. On the film shot on the day prior to the heist by the Asda store's own cameras, police homed in on an individual who was seen to be studiously surveying the store and taking notes as he went. Perhaps he was simply a shopper who paid particular attention to detail but police and store management were confident they had caught sight of somebody who was at least part of the gang responsible. The suspect was one of the few positive leads for police to follow early in the investigation and it reiterated the premeditation involved. It was organised and determined, designed to bring maximum return in the quickest possible time.

What was needed more than anything else was information from the public, particularly from those who knew the gang responsible. To entice that type of disclosure, they used the currency most recognised by that particular fraternity – with officials at Asda quick to offer a reward. There was £30,000 on offer for information leading to the conviction of the raiders but the cash incentive did little to help improve the flow of information and police turned to new avenues in their efforts to crack the case.

As a firm, Asda has a well-worn policy for dealing with

such incidents and it was not slow to react. Retail success has brought unwanted problems for the firm, which has found itself being targeted by those keen to take a slice of the profits for themselves. Perhaps the most high-profile of all was the heist that never happened, when the Flying Squad swooped in 2006 to foil an attempted £1-million robbery at an Asda store in Leyton, East London. The gang responsible had gained access to the cash room and were set to make their getaway when they were apprehended in the car park.

Unfortunately for police in Edinburgh, they had not had prior warning of the attack on The Jewel. Two months after the robbery, the episode was featured on the BBC's *Crimewatch* programme as police desperately tried to keep the trail warm. The impact of that appeal was heightened by the screening of the security camera video capturing the moment the Vauxhall ploughed into the store, sending debris flying and staff running for cover. Whilst the two main protagonists were masked, there was enough detail to issue an e-fit image of the getaway driver – an olive-skinned man in his early 30s with a distinctive mark on his left cheek. Traditionally, e-fit has been a hit-and-miss approach to detection but, in the absence of a better or more reliable tool, it was deemed to be worth a shot.

Inspector Harry McAdam, who was leading the investigation for Lothian and Borders Police, said at the time: 'These were ruthless men who cared nothing about the safety of members of the public and were only interested in money. The two members of staff were very lucky that they were not seriously injured or even killed as the car smashed through the doors. They literally were just seconds away from tragedy.'

McAdam was a bullish presence in the force and cut a committed figure as he set about seeking out the offenders. He was in charge of a substantial group of officers, with resources poured into the case.

In response to the *Crimewatch* appeal, more than 80 calls were made by viewers following the broadcast – 30 of those to Lothian and Borders Police and 50 to the expert team of call handlers in the London studio – with many of those people offering names for members of the gang. Importantly, several names were mentioned more than once to give solid foundations for the next stage. Information on a suspicious vehicle seen in the car park of the store around the time of the raid was also provided. Every single one of those 80 calls was logged and followed up as part of the meticulous bid to leave no stone unturned.

Although seen by millions who watched the horrifying CCTV footage played out on *Crimewatch*, the two employees never spoke at length in public about their ordeal. Management at the superstore revealed the pair were too traumatised by their experiences and were undergoing counselling. They had endured a twin-pronged attack. The shock of the near miss with the car at the point of impact would have been enough to make an indelible mark on anyone's memory but the life-or-death scenario presented by the gun-toting thugs who had come crashing into their lives added to the trauma. The security guards admitted they thought the raiders were going to open fire.

According to experts in the field, emotions such as anger and fear are common among victims of crime. Physical signs can include insomnia or a general feeling of illness. Asda's support for its employees and the acknowledgment of the value of counselling in the healing process entirely met the recommendations of organisations such as Victim Support which insists that the crucial aspect for anyone in that situation is to be aware of the traumatic experience they have encountered and the way in which it will shape their feelings. What is also undisputed is that the impact can be long lasting for those who have had the misfortune of being at the centre of an incident similar to the raid at The Jewel.

The *Crimewatch* footage enabled Britain's viewing public to witness the speed and brutality with which the robbers struck and to appreciate the likely impact that it would have had on the staff caught up in it. The hope was that sympathy and the harsh reality of the CCTV images might shock someone into coming forward with new information.

At that stage, a new strand was revealed by police. The probe moved in a new direction and, for the first time, evidence suggested the investigating team held a strong hand. The false number plates recovered from the Cavalier were to become central to the investigation. With strict guidelines governing the supply of car registration plates in place, it should not, in theory, be possible for false plates to be made, but for those determined to bend the law it is far from difficult. However, police in Edinburgh were able to identify the origin of the plates recovered at Newcraighall Drive – and it was not in a local garage. Instead, they were tracked back to Newcastle which, in time, would take on greater significance. With the raid having been carried out on the south of the city and in the vicinity of the A1, the main road from Edinburgh to Newcastle, it appeared all roads did, indeed, lead to Tyneside, where the ram-raiding scene had been in full flow for a number of years.

With the English link to the Edinburgh raid established through the numberplates, forces south of the Border took a close interest in the case. It became part of Operation Solar – an all-encompassing probe into a series of 10 supermarket attacks over the course of around a year in locations throughout the north of England and, through the Edinburgh incident, into Scotland. That operation came to fruition when eight men and one woman were arrested in dawn raids led by West Yorkshire Police, at the same time involving intelligence from seven other forces. Incidents in Northumbria, Yorkshire and Northamptonshire were among those under scrutiny. Around 90 police officers were enlisted to carry out the raids at 16 locations in Northumbria and South Yorkshire, with the suspects apprehended and taken to Leeds for questioning.

It brought to an end that particular operation but not the chosen method of attack. Ram raids have continued to provide some of the most dramatic visual prompts in Scottish criminal investigations. In 2012, two robbers earned notoriety when CCTV images of their attempts to rob an HSBC base in South Lanarkshire were beamed around the world.

Using a stolen sewage tanker as their vehicle of choice, the duo careered through glass doors at the bank's call centre in

Blantyre and towards an ATM machine inside. Despite the drama of the incident, it was ultimately unsuccessful. George Nicol and David Fowler were both subsequently arrested and brought to justice. Nicol had been the driver of the tanker whilst Fowler, driving the Skoda Octavia getaway car, had followed behind and was armed with a sawn-off shotgun. They had attempted to smash open the ATM with a sledgehammer after making their entrance using the truck but fled empty-handed and were captured after a police chase.

Although not profitable for two culprits, it was an expensive business for HSBC and the owners of the tanker which had been taken from East Kilbride. The bank had to pay close to £200,000 to repair the damage. The truck's owners estimated it would cost £50,000 to replace the vehicle and they also lost out on up to £60,000 in business in the interim period.

As he sat in front of the accused, Judge Lord Glennie described the raid was as 'bizarre' and said, 'The only saving grace in this case is that the crime was carried out in such an incompetent fashion.'

Both men were jailed. Nicol's defence team told the court that their client, a former garage owner, had turned to crime to compensate for financial difficulties. His story was similar to Fowler's – he had lost his job prior to the incident. Nicol's solicitor Paul Nelson told the court: 'The video footage shows the inept nature of the crime. It is a demonstrable fact that the person who committed the crime is monumentally stupid or desperate. He is not stupid. He was quite desperate.'

The difference between the Blantyre two and the Edinburgh ram-raid gang was the level of planning and, in cold hard terms, the end result. The Asda gang got in and out without being caught and sped away from the scene to the sanctuary of England along the A1, a path that is well trodden by criminals from south of the border who view the link as an open invitation. That was demonstrated in 2004 when a trio from Leeds were jailed for a combined period of 42 years – after being snared by virtue of their smallest misdemeanour.

Tam Lamb, Anthony Waite and James Weaver thought they

had escaped detection when they attacked two security van crew members outside a branch of the Abbey National building society on Edinburgh's affluent Morningside Road. Armed with a shotgun and baseball bat, they terrorised the shocked delivery men as they arrived to stock up the branch's cash machine.

It later transpired the same trio had been behind a similar raid in Bournemouth, netting £90,000 between the two incidents. However, their forward planning proved to be their downfall. During a reconnaissance visit to the capital, their trusty getaway car – a silver Jaguar – had been slapped with a parking ticket whilst left in the Bruntsfield district of the city.

They returned on 3 March 2003, to carry out their robbery. Bundling two of the Securicor team into the entrance of the bank, they grabbed the cash cases they were carrying. Inside was £58,000. The gang ran off into Springvalley Gardens, picking up the Jaguar and making off through the city. The car was found abandoned and burning in Monkwood Court.

Because of the earlier parking ticket, police were able to piece together the movements of the gang and found they had stayed at nearby hotels, using false names to book their rooms, during the planning stages. It also helped establish a link to incidents elsewhere in Britain. Lothian and Borders Police Detective Sergeant Jerry Fraser revealed at the time: 'These are very serious crimes. It was very traumatic for the security guards as the robbers were using real guns. They were a serious bunch of people.

'We worked out that the gang had made at least three visits to Edinburgh before the robbery. We knew that the getaway car had been stolen in Leeds. We then found out that a parking ticket had been put on the car in a street in Bruntsfield during one of the gang's visits.

'The car was similar to one being used in crimes up and down the country. We also traced them to a hotel in Bruntsfield. All the evidence was pointing to the Leeds connection so we had to work with West Yorkshire Police to prove that this gang had been up here. The work that West Yorkshire Police put into this is amazing.'

Their trial was held at Leeds Crown Court in December 2004 and, at the end of three weeks of evidence, Lamb was sentenced to 16 years in prison with Waite and Weaver each told to serve 13 years despite all denying the charges. A fourth member of the gang was never arrested. Prosecutors said 'perfect planning and professional execution' had been features of the robberies and it was later confirmed that Lamb was already serving a nine-year term for his part in a Leeds supermarket robbery in 1999.

As the superstore sector boomed through the 1990s and into the 2000s, it stood to reason that crime rates increased in parallel. More open than banks yet, in many cases, just as cash-laden, they were prime targets. The raid on the Asda store at The Jewel in Edinburgh was a particularly severe example and that store was no stranger to other incidents, particularly in the years following the armed ram raid. From a bus being stolen by joyriders outside the shop to an armed response unit being scrambled to deal with what turned out to be a group of youngsters brandishing a ball-bearing gun, it has seen it all. In one incident, a security man clung on for his life on the bonnet of a car as a suspected shoplifter sped off.

It will, however, forever be associated with what, for more than a decade and a half, was the biggest cash robbery Scotland's capital city had seen.

11

Blood on the Streets

The discovery of the dead body in the commercial heart of Edinburgh caused shock, repulsion and horror and the fact that the murderer was motivated by nothing more than greed made the crime even more sickening.

It was not a robbery gone wrong – it was a deadly accurate plan carried out to the letter. The outcome was one deceased bank employee and one raider, who was rich beyond his wildest dreams, escaping with enough cash to last a lifetime.

The heinous crime took place just yards from the safe haven of one of the capital's best-known and most respected financial institutions but, at the same time, exposed glaring gaps in that same organisation's security procedures.

To understand those deficiencies, the trail leading to the tragic end has to be followed from the start. It began with the routine of the daily collection of money from a network of branches along a designated route in Edinburgh. The route began in Leith and continued across North Bridge towards the High Street and Canongate areas on the homeward stretch towards headquarters. On a cold winter's afternoon, at the end of a busy banking day in which tellers had been busily filling vaults, the familiar cash run began.

On this November day, what the bank worker entrusted with the responsibility of leading that exercise did not realise was that his every move was being watched. He moved along the trail he had followed countless times before, little realising that the industry he built his life around was the same industry which would end that life prematurely.

The robber was patient and was determined. He waited until his target was briefly out of sight, nearing his destination, and struck with a brutish and premeditated force which has rarely been seen on the streets of a Scottish city.

The level of pre-planning and thought was demonstrated by the murder weapon, which was recovered at the scene. The victim had been stabbed in the chest and the knife was left embedded, with a piece of paper very deliberately slid up the blade and resting at the handle. The reason? To prevent the killer being splattered with blood when he carried out his fatal attack and, therefore, aiding his chances of a clean getaway, in the knowledge he would be making his departure on foot through streets busy with pedestrians.

The body of the bank employee was found soon after the murderer had struck, at around 5 p.m. The money he had been carrying on the final leg of his daily assignment was not recovered – it was long gone. And that was what lay at the root of the slaying – cash. Even in today's era of fantastic plastic, it is still cold hard money that makes the world go round. And, for as long as there is currency in circulation, there will be opportunities for criminals to profit. As long as there are criminals fuelled by greed there will be a real threat to those entrusted with safeguarding the funds of bank customers. But this heist was not one from the era of debit and credit cards. The fateful date was 13 November 1806 and the amount stolen was £4,392 – an unimaginable bounty given the two centuries of inflation which have passed since that time.

The vicious raider had not been trailing one of today's armoured security vans but a humble bank messenger who made his cash run on foot with all the reliability of a metronome. William Begbie carried with him a yellow bag, standard issue from the British Linen Bank at which he worked. Despite his high-value package, he had nothing with which to defend himself in the event of a robbery. That day, he had made the walk from the British Linen Bank branch in Leith, then a bustling port packed with merchants and a hub of activity. It was a centre for legitimate trading but also a point of entry for smugglers and those with shadier motives. Whilst today Leith is considered part of Edinburgh life, in the 1800s it was very much a settlement in its own right. The walk into the city was not the fluent connection it now is, with Leith Walk described in those days as a stark and, at times, dangerous path to tread.

The British Linen Bank's presence was an example of the self-sufficiency Leith boasted of. The Commercial Bank, National Bank, Union Bank, Clydesdale Bank and Bank of Scotland also set up shop in the port too in a bid to service the commerce which went with the hustle and bustle of the area. There were also three newspapers in the area, a collection of hotels and inns as well as representation from nations as far afield as Brazil, Russia and Turkey through consuls posted to the seaside location.

It was in Leith that Begbie, unbeknown to him, attracted the attention of the man who would take his life from him. Dressed all in black, the killer followed his prey up Leith Walk, along Leith Street, across Waterloo Place and then over North Bridge to the High Street, Canongate and on into Tweeddale Court. The small passageway led to the British Linen Bank's main base in Edinburgh, and for Begbie this was the home stretch of his journey; but he never made it to his destination.

Under the cover of the close, he was stabbed and left for dead by his assailant who had vanished by the time the body was discovered. What made the murder all the more horrific was that the first person on the scene was a young girl, who had been sent by her mother to fetch a kettle of water from a nearby well. Her house was accessed by an entrance from the close and she found Begbie as he drew his last breath.

Police in the capital were left to pick over a horrific scene but, at a time long before the idea of forensics had been invented, it was very much a basic assessment and a search for physical clues. CSI Edinburgh it certainly was not. Even the concept of fingerprinting to aid identification did not appear in the law enforcer's toolkit until more than a century later, so options for investigation were limited. If you weren't captured red-handed, the chances of detection were slim – making Edinburgh in that period in history a criminal's playground.

The Edinburgh Police Act of 1805, just a year before the murder, had sought to make life more difficult for those who insisted on breaching the laws of the land. It brought the reorganisation of the city's police force, with an emphasis on a more efficient network of watchmen linked to a network of 52 police boxes throughout the capital. Each watchman would patrol a beat surrounding their own box, supervised by a greater number of sergeants in recognition of the increasing challenge of keeping citizens safe. It was far more advanced than the system in play across the country in Glasgow, where everything was handled from one central police office. But the focus was very much on night watchmen. During the day, there were far fewer watchmen and it was during business hours that Begbie's killer had struck. Notably, he had chosen to strike in a public place, perhaps mindful of the fact that a force known as the City Guard provided armed protection for the banks to ward off the threat of robbery.

The killing of Begbie, who left behind a wife and four children, hadn't been detected whilst in progress. What those investigating the crime desperately needed were eyewitness accounts but nobody, it appeared, had witnessed the ultimate end to the robbery and few came forward with any useful information on the minutes leading up to that moment.

Today, Tweeddale Court can still be found – part of the well-worn tourist trail surrounding the Royal Mile. From the exterior, with its decorative crest and lovingly painted detailing in shades of green, maroon and gold, it looks like a quaint corner of the city but it hides a dark and terrible history which few of the visitors from far and near will ever discover as they meander towards Edinburgh Castle.

That is, of course, unless they are specifically looking for that particular spot. In the quest to find a niche in the tourism market, a variety of walking tours have sprung up in the capital, taking in everything from the standard landmarks

to the more ghoulish sites the city has to offer. The scene of
Begbie's unfortunate demise has found its way onto some of
those tours and even appears on the itinerary of trails listed in
traditional tourist handbooks. It is a macabre attraction but a
lure nonetheless.

The entrance to the lane retains its original features, complete with nameplate and wrought-iron gates to ward off unde-
sirables. It also still has the shelter used for the sedan chairs
which were used to carry the wealthier citizens through the city
streets. Closes are common sights, with more than 75 in the
vicinity of the Royal Mile alone. Many have been preserved in
some shape or form, offering a glimpse of the past and a hint
of the warren-like nature of Edinburgh in days gone by. At
the time of Begbie's death the streets, on a dark afternoon in
midwinter, would have been dimly lit by gas lamps – making
the closes even more gloomy.

What Tweeddale Court did then was to provide a fleeting,
tantalising sight of what it provides access to – the magnificent
mansion which in 1806 was head office of the British Linen
bank. Throughout the day messengers would scurry through
the close to deposit the bags of cash they had collected from
branches throughout the city, always returning to the impressive surroundings of their base.

Tweeddale House, as it was christened, was once home to
Dame Margaret Kerr, daughter of the 1st Earl of Lothian,
but has seen various guises since it was first built in the
16th century. Over time, it was extended, remodelled and
revamped to carry it through various stages of its life as a
residential and business property. In the 1750s it underwent
considerable transformation, and in 1791 the British Linen
Bank moved in.

The bank was a new kid on the block in many ways. Having
been involved in banking since the 1760s, it was not part of the
industry's establishment but was beginning to thrive. By 1800,
it was said to have had 18 branches and, in the century that
followed, that number snowballed. It later became part of the
Barclays family of companies and in 1969 was sold to the Bank

of Scotland. The name continued to be used for the merchant arm of the business, finally disappearing completely in 1999.

The bank remained at Tweeddale Court for a further 11 years after the death of Begbie and employees had to walk past the scene of the death of one of their friends and colleagues every day as they reported for duty. In 1817, they moved out and publisher Oliver and Boyd took up residence. That business remained in place until 1973. Today there is a mix of commercial and residential use, with *The List* magazine among the tenants of this intriguing corner of Edinburgh. The macabre events of 1806 play a major part in its infamy and still feature in everything from tourist guides to property schedules – the passage of time apparently making the crime palatable to the point of it almost becoming a badge of honour rather than a mark of shame.

At the time, however, the opposite was true and genuine shock was matched by intrigue when it came to the case of William Begbie and news-sheets – or 'broadsides' as they were known – ensured the public were well aware of what had happened. It is easy to take for granted the incredible array of news platforms today, from 24-hour news channels to Twitter and other online sites. Edinburgh at the turn of the 19th century was very different – *The Scotsman* was not even a twinkle in the eye of William Ritchie, who launched that particular title in 1817 to serve the city. A plethora of news-sheets was prominent on the streets of the capital as printers began to branch out into news gathering and publishing.

Within hours of Begbie's death, flyers with the story, hot off the press, were being handed out as word spread throughout the surrounding area and further afield. One headline announced: out: 'HUE AND CRY – ATROCIOUS MURDER AND ROBBERY'. The report appealed to anyone who had sold 'a common bread knife' to a suspicious figure in the build-up to the date in question to report to police. The murder weapon was a wooden-handled knife, with that handle stained a red colour at the time of manufacture. To highlight the premeditation involved, it was later revealed that the rounded tip of the knife had been ground to a point in what was viewed as an attempt to make the weapon more deadly.

The hope was that those extra details would provoke a response, especially when coupled with a 500-guinea reward which was being offered in return for information leading to a conviction. In addition, those in authority were offering immunity from prosecution for any accomplices who came forward to name the murderer. Reports also detailed the types of notes and the denominations which had been stolen – those in question were marked with the name of Sir William Forbes and Company as well as the Leith Banking Company and various other institutions of the era – to ensure that banks and other institutions knew what to be on the lookout for. The report stated: 'It is intreated that bankers, merchants, and others will take notice of all notes of the above Descriptions which may happen to be presented to them, especially if by persons of suspicious appearance.'

Yet the plea to bankers and the financial incentive of the reward did not bring the clues that would resolve the mystery. With little to go on, there was no significant leap forward in the investigation until almost a year later. Known criminals in Edinburgh had been searched in the immediate aftermath of the robbery but that was to no avail. Not a single note had been found in or around Edinburgh until, on 10 August 1807, three men discovered a package hidden in the Bellevue area of the city. As they unwrapped it, they discovered £3,000 in British Linen Bank notes. Resisting temptation and displaying admirable honesty, they immediately reported their find to bank officials and were presented with a £200 reward for their efforts. It was not a patch on the haul they had returned but was still a noteworthy sum for the trio.

Bank chiefs had given up any hope of seeing the money again so, when three quarters of the original cash landed back on their counter, they were understandably pleased. With that money in the vault, interest in pursuing the culprit waned somewhat and, as regrettable as it may sound, life went on as the months and years passed.

At one stage, a man who was said to be of 'great physical strength' and 'desperate' character was apprehended and held in custody. Although he had been in the Canongate area at the time of the murder, it transpired that it had been on other criminal business and eventually he was released having served his time on remand. Others were also grilled in great depth but the likely suspects were all found to have alibis which stood up to the closest scrutiny. Every turn for police presented a dead end.

That was until, more than a decade later, fresh evidence was presented which appeared to bring clarity to the cloudy waters of the case, which had been stirred up by speculation and assumption. It transpired that one key witness had not been traced at the time – a man who believed he had seen most of the activity which had led to the eventual stabbing, albeit not the final act itself. Concerned that some illicit smuggling of his own on that fateful day would come to light, he had not come forward at the time but, eventually, his description of events was heard and brought to court as a name was put to the prime suspect – a man known as James Mackcoull or James Moffat. By the time he came forward, the witness was a respected teacher and his standing in the local community added weight to his account of the fateful day. Back then, he had been a merchant seaman – a young man making his way in the world – and was not aware he held the key to unlock the answer to one of his country's major crimes.

Although sentenced to be executed in 1820 after being captured in relation to a heist in Glasgow, Mackcoull failed to make it to the gallows and died in mysterious circumstances in his cell at Calton Prison. His demise meant there would be no closure as far Begbie's death and the subsequent theft of money were concerned. Mackcoull had always protested his innocence of the Edinburgh crime and reviews of the case have concluded that judges felt there had not been enough hard evidence to be sure of his guilt. To this day, nobody really knows the true story.

While there was no full stop to end that violent chapter in

Edinburgh's history plenty has been written in the interim to add colour to the story. The most detailed account was published in 1820, in what would have been the equivalent of today's tabloid newspapers, and has been preserved in the National Library of Scotland's archives, where experts have described the account as 'a peculiar broadside' which 'sensationally claims to answer the riddle' of Begbie's death. Although based on circumstantial evidence gathered from accounts of the criminal fraternity and other witnesses, it is the closest there has been to a full explanation.

The piece used a memorandum from the 1820 court proceedings as its basis, with the transcript reading:

In the autumn of 1805, Mackcoull made his daily appearance in the Ship Tavern in Leith, and gave himself out for a British Merchant fled from Hamburgh when the French took possession of that place. He spoke German a little, but upon questioning it was easily found he was no merchant. Mackcoull frequented the ship tavern for about 12 months, and immediately disappeared after the murder was committed.

A sailor, who is now a respectable schoolmaster in Leith, had come home from Lisbon, and having some small present which he brought to his mother, he left Leith with it on the night of the murder – and when on his road, he saw a tall man with a yellow bag under his arm going up the Walk, who he supposed was a smuggler, but who was Begbie, and a man dogging after him, who he supposed was an Excise officer. For fear of his own little present, which was seizable, he put it into his breast and keeped behind them watching the officer's motions.

Sailors of the era were accustomed to playing a game of cat and mouse with the excise men who patrolled Leith's port, looking out for the import of any items which should not have been brought into the country – at least, not without appropriate tax being paid. It would not have been uncommon to see that played out on the city's streets but the witness had got it wrong as Begbie was no smuggler – he was an honest bank worker. And his pursuer, darting in and out of the shadows, or 'dogging' as it was termed, in an attempt not to be seen by the man he was tailing, was far from an upstanding member of the Excise team. He was a murderer in waiting.

The transcript continued by explaining that the star witness had lost sight of the duo at the head of North Bridge and continued on his way up High Street, picking up the trail a short time later. It stated:

> Just as he came opposite the bank close he saw the officer coming running out of it with something below his coat, and being afraid of losing his own he made haste to his mother's and delivered the present, and then went direct to Leith, from whence he sailed in a day or two, and was taken by the French, and kept in prison until after the peace.

That imprisonment explained the lengthy gap between the murder and the evidence filtering into the public domain.

The testimony also drew parallels between the clothing Mackcoull was said to have been wearing and that worn by the person seen following Begbie. It also pieced together other key factors which were used to point towards the prime suspect's guilt. The transcript explained:

> Mackcoull always left Leith about dusk to go to his lodgings at the foot of New Street and the murderer ran down Leith Wynd, whence he could easily make to New Street by bye entries. Mackcoull did not make his appearance till 12 months afterwards, and his constant walk was down by Bellevue, where the large notes were found about the same period. Mackcoull immediately changed his lodgings to a quite different airt.

The circumstantial picture being painted was powerful but, without a confession, there was little prospect of a conviction or satisfactory judgement on who had truly killed Begbie ever being made.

While Mackcoull awaited trial, one of his associates visited him in prison, in an attempt to tease an admission from him.

He failed but the account of that encounter does add more flavour to the somewhat bizarre elements of the investigation. The transcript states:

> Mackcoull resided in a remote house beside Boston the gardener, to avoid suspicion. The same gentleman (Boston) called at the prison after Mackcoull's condemnation, and taking advantage of his situation, conversed with him for some time in his cell in presence of the Governor [Captain Sibbald].
>
> He told Captain Sibbald he intended to ask the prisoner a single question relative to the murder of Begbie, but would first humour him with a few jokes, so as to throw him off his guard, and prevent him from thinking that he called on him for any particular purpose, but desired Captain Sibbald to watch the features of the prisoner when he put his hand to his chin, for he would then put the question he meant.
>
> After talking for some time on different topics, he put this very simple question to the prisoner: 'By the way, Mackcoull, if I am correct, you resided at the foot of New Street, Canongate, in November, 1806, did you not?' He stared, he rolled his eyes and, as if falling into a convulsion, threw himself back on his bed! In this position he continued for a few moments, when as if recollecting himself, he started up, exclaiming wildly: 'No! I was then in the East Indies? In the West Indies... what do you mean?'
>
> 'I mean no harm Mackcoull, I merely asked the question for my own curiosity, for I think when you left these lodgings you went to Dublin, is it not so?'
>
> 'Yes, yes, I went to Dublin – and I wish I had remained there still? I won L 10,000 there at the tables, and never knew what it was to want cash.'

According to the detailed account, Mackcoull then seemed to 'rave and lose all temper' and the visit was over. The amateur inquisitor made his way back out, perhaps a little more confident in his own assertion that his acquaintance had some role to play but without the cast-iron proof or confession he had hoped would bring the case to an end once and for all.

There was, however, a groundswell of opinion that Mackcoull was the guilty party. He was described in newspaper reports as a 'London rogue of unparalleled effrontery and dexterity' who, for years, had 'haunted Scotland' and carried out some 'daring robberies'. He was said to be a gambler and a pick-pocket. Whether that made him guilty of this bloody heist we will never know.

12

A City's Darkest Day

They were described as 'the gentlemen raiders' following their first heist but, by the end of their second, two dedicated police officers lay dead on what has been described as one of the darkest days in the history of the service in Glasgow. The gang responsible were anything but gentlemanly.

The cold-blooded murders of acting Detective Constable Angus MacKenzie and Police Constable Edward Barnett in a flat on the city's Allison Street, as they closed in on a group of bank robbers, remains one of the most brutal and horrific incidents ever witnessed on Clydeside. MacKenzie and Barnett both died after being shot in the head and their colleague, Inspector Andrew Hyslop, was left paralysed after a bullet lodged in his skull.

The senseless killings took place on 30 December 1969, in the immediate aftermath of a £14,000 heist at the Linwood branch of the Clydesdale Bank that same day. The seeds, however, were sown months earlier, when the same men first acquired their taste for armed robbery.

Rewind back to the summer of '69. In Glasgow, it was not one which would be immortalised for the right reasons but, rather, for the start of a crime wave which ended in tragedy. It was 16 July – a sun-kissed afternoon on Scotland's west coast but one to endure rather than enjoy for the staff at the British Linen Bank in the Glasgow suburb of Williamwood. It was and still is a prosperous area, with a bustling village feel and part of a chain of well-cared-for towns and villages to the south of the city in the thriving commuter belt. The fact that

Giffnock, Newton Mearns, Clarkston and Williamwood are all just a 15-minute drive away from the city centre may have been regarded as a blessing to its residents but, on this occasion, it proved to be a curse as the easy access represented a major attraction to the raiders. The branch, along with a clutch of shops and businesses, sat proudly on the main road, Eastwoodmains Road.

It was late afternoon when three men walked into the neatly presented bank and subjected the employees to a traumatic ordeal. The trio, smartly dressed and described by witnesses as looking like auditors, drew no suspicious glances as they entered but the mood quickly changed as they barked out their orders at the team behind the counter. They were armed with guns and the threat that they would use them was key to their plan.

Bank manager Len Archibald, his assistant David Gowans and clerks Ian Shaw and Helga Muirhead were bound, gagged and blindfolded before having pillowcases tied over their heads. They were then forced into the bank's back office and kept under guard. The single telephone line in the building was cut by the raiders for added safety as they set about filling briefcases full of used banknotes. Within 15 minutes, they had walked back out of the front door with close to £20,000 in cash. They left behind the terrified bank staff, still helpless in the manager's cramped office. It was only when Ian Shaw managed to free himself from the bindings which held his arms and legs together that the alarm was raised, with the desperate clerk fleeing to a neighbouring newsagent's shop and using their phone to alert police.

Within 24 hours 70 officers had been allocated to the case, with the Renfrewshire force's operation led by Detective Chief Superintendent James Ferrie. They flooded into the area of the raid, speaking to those who worked in businesses surrounding the compact branch and going from door to door in a bid to move the investigation forward.

It was an era in which policing was far more localised than today and not yet under the centralised Police Scotland model or the previous regionalised incarnation of the network of forces. Renfrew and Bute Constabulary – an organisation which served the area through to 1975 when it and the other local units were swallowed up to create the new Strathclyde Police – was left to run the show. It did not have the same crime rate or type of incidents to deal with as the likes of the neighbouring Glasgow City force but plenty of experienced and skilled officers were assigned to the case.

Banks were in the midst of ongoing security reviews at that time, regularly publishing updated information for staff to detail the expected response when confronted by raiders. Just prior to the Williamwood heist, the National Union of Bank Employees had also issued guidance to workers at every branch on how to treat injuries caused by ammonia attacks. A union representative said: 'We would not divulge what the banks are doing in matters of security, but we are greatly concerned about the increasing number of hold-ups. We are continually having talks with the banks about protective measures.'

Despite the police resources being ploughed into the investigation, the probe drew a blank. Unfortunately, the raiders did not quit whilst they were ahead and, by the festive season of 1969, they were back. On 30 December the crew chose to strike, singling out the Clydesdale Bank in Linwood, Renfrew. Again, the location was to the south-west of Glasgow and, once more, it was not a quiet area as the town, at that time, was buoyed by the production of cars at the Hillman factory which had opened just six years earlier.

The location was not particularly unusual but what was notable was that this was not a spontaneous act – they had, in fact, made an appointment. One member of the group had called at the Bridge Street branch and spoken to a member of staff about meeting with the manager to open an account for a new plant hire business. It was a perfectly plausible story and it was agreed that he would return the following day with two associates to complete the formalities.

The motley crew were true to their word, reporting the following day and asking for the manager. He was not available so the bank's accountant showed the men to a back office to allow them to wait. As he led them into the room he was bundled to the floor and had a gun held to his head. He was told by his attacker, 'Listen, you will hear me release the safety catch.' And he did – there was a click as the pistol was primed.

A second raider, armed with a dagger, held a blade to his throat and said, 'If we have your full co-operation, no members of your staff will come to any harm.'

When the bank manager arrived on the scene, he met with similar treatment. Then it was the turn of the three members of staff and a customer. Each was shepherded into the back office, a pillowcase was pulled over their heads and their arms and legs bound. The doors of the bank were locked to allow the gang to fill the suitcases they had brought with them – but there was a problem.

A customer was trying to get in and wasn't taking no for an answer. The young woman knocked at the door and was ignored. She knocked again and was ignored again. Eventually, worried that the excluded customer would be becoming con-spicuous out on the street during opening hours, the door was opened and she was allowed in. She was greeted not with the usual nod and smile from staff but by a pistol being held to her head by a robber.

There was another problem. She had parked her two-year-old son in his pram outside the branch. Again, the door was opened and she was ordered to wheel the youngster's pram into the building. It must have been a moment of sheer terror for the frightened young mum who, together with her boy, was forced to join the other captives as the heist unfolded. One of the clerks was untied and, at knifepoint, made to open the safe and money drawers to enable unhindered access for the assailants. As this was going on, the brave young customer who had become embroiled in the horrific scenario made attempts to untie members of staff. When one of the robbers returned to the back room and discovered what was happening, he held a gun to her head and that of her two-year-old child. Fortunately for them, he did not follow through with his threat to shoot.

Despite the interruptions and unexpected twist, the gang succeeded in what they had set out to achieve and, carrying £14,212 with them, they exited a short time later. They also took with them a large heavy metal box stuffed full of coins. That had been an afterthought, with the notes the main interest until one of the gang spotted the mountain of silver. With the cash stashed in the suitcases and the metal box disguised by being placed in a cardboard box, the team of robbers made their way back to Govanhill on the south side of the Clyde in their getaway car. They calmly parked on Allison Street, a typical inner-city residential road, and began to unload the car's contents. There was no reason for anyone to suspect anything untoward – unless, of course, that someone was trained to think about and query anything that appeared even slightly unusual.

Inspector Andrew Hyslop was in the area and not only saw the car being emptied, he also instantly recognised the man leading the cargo operation. That man was Howard Wilson who at one stage had been a member of the police force. Hyslop knew him from that time but was suspicious of him and the path he had followed after leaving the force at the end of 10 years' service. Something struck a chord with Hyslop as he watched from a distance, even though news of the bank robbery had yet to filter through. He sent out a radio message for back-up from colleagues, before moving closer to the flat where the car was parked. He was spotted by Wilson and invited in on friendly terms. Once inside, the tone changed as Hyslop asked to take a look inside one of the suitcases. As the lid was peeled back and Hyslop was greeted with the sight of bundles of banknotes, Wilson pulled out a gun and held it to his visitor's head. As he pulled the trigger, the mechanism jammed but a second shot fired and caused irrevocable damage. Hyslop survived but he was paralysed.

Fellow officers John Sellars, Angus MacKenzie and Edward Barnett came rushing into the flat to Hyslop's aid but Wilson was in no mood to surrender. MacKenzie and Barnett were both shot in the head but Sellars was able to escape to the safety of the flat's bathroom. MacKenzie was still alive after the first shot. Wilson prepared to finish the job he had started and was standing over his victim ready to fire when Detective Constable John Campbell interrupted, barging into the room and diving towards the gunman. The final bullet left in the chamber was sent soaring into the ceiling.

Both MacKenzie and Barnett went on to die from their injuries, with Hyslop bearing his scars – physical and mental – right up to his death in 2000. He was 74 when he passed away but the pain of that day had never faded.

Hyslop was steeped in the tradition of law and order. His father had been a policeman in Glasgow and, after completing his National Service, he proudly followed in his dad's footsteps. His career began with the Metropolitan Police in London before he transferred to the City of Glasgow force, where he rose to become a sergeant and was instrumental in introducing firearms training. One of the constables enlisted in that pro-gramme was Howard Wilson. The death of Hyslop brought the horror of Wilson's crimes back in focus, not least for those still involved in police duties. Officers from the Strathclyde force carried Hyslop's coffin in a mark of solidarity and respect for one of their forefathers, a symbolic gesture of togetherness for men who appreciated his honour and integrity. It was in stark contrast to the feelings for Wilson among those who wore the uniform he himself had once donned when in the force.

The ease with which the callous killer was able to get his hands on the weapon used was very much a sign of the times. Today, in the wake of the Dunblane massacre, legislation helps guard against the use of handguns for illicit purposes but in 1970 controls were far less rigorous.

Wilson and his accomplices, Ian Donaldson and John Sim, were all members of a shooting club in Bearsden, where they could put their skills to test on the range. They legally purchased a Vostok .22 pistol from an office-bearer at the club in a deal that later was to have bloody consequences. It was a Russian-made gun popular on the target shooting circuit and known for its reliability and accuracy. Dating as far back as the 1940s, this same basic design is still being used more than 60 years on.

Wilson stood trial in 1970. He admitted the murders and was sentenced to 25 years in jail. John Sim and Ian Donaldson were both sent to prison for 12 years after being found guilty of being involved in the robberies. Wilson was sent to the notoriously tough Peterhead Prison – a former policeman in amongst Scotland toughest criminals. He was far from a model inmate. His sentence was increased by six years after he was convicted, along with others, of bidding to escape from prison and attempting to kill six prison officers during a rooftop protest. He was moved to a special segregation unit at Porterfield Prison in the aftermath. The Peterhead incident, in 1972, was a headline-grabbing act by the inmates but ultimately was a futile effort. The men involved had luxuries such as television access removed and were left in no doubt that they would not get the better of the prison service.

Meanwhile, both the Clydesdale Bank and the British Linen Bank turned to the courts to recover the money stolen from them and each was granted a decree against the raiders for the sum of £16,446 in the case of the BLB and £14,000 for the Clydesdale. It was a move which followed the letter of the law but, in reality, was never likely to reunite either of the organisations with their missing money. Those involved had already proved they weren't keen to comply with instruction from authority.

Later, after a disruptive start to prison life, Wilson discovered a passion for writing, penning *Angels of Death*, a novel which won the Koestler Award for prisoners who embrace the arts. The book, published in 1994, tells the story of a private investigator who once had a promising police career on the trail of a serial killer. It encompasses a ruthless mob, a religious cult and heavy-duty drug dealers. In part, at least, it sounds as though art may be imitating life for the killer-turned-author.

Wilson, with that book already under his belt, was released in 2002 at the age of 64, after serving 33 years. The Scottish government, conscious of the likely backlash, made it clear that the Parole Board had made the decision based on a full and frank assessment of the risk posed by the killer to public safety.

The Scottish Police Federation was critical of the decision to release the prisoner, insisting any release was too early. Norrie Flowers, the chairman of the federation at that time, said: 'This was a pretty horrific case, even though it was 32 years ago. When you look at it from the perspective that this was a former police officer who murdered two police officers, and attempted to murder another police officer, there were three ruined lives. We just feel that anyone who murders a police officer should never be released. Life should mean life. The relatives of all the people that were murdered have got a life sentence of their own to deal with, so we think at the very least the killer should also serve that sentence.'

Thankfully, fatal attacks on serving police officers in Scotland have been rare. Some have lost their lives in road traffic accidents but the type of violence witnessed in Allison Street has not been the norm. There have been incidents since then which have rocked the west coast, not least the death of PC George Taylor in November 1976. He was the first officer to be killed on duty following the formation of Strathclyde Police. On a routine patrol near the State Hospital in Carstairs, he and a colleague stumbled upon two men, dressed as prison officers, who, they felt, were acting suspiciously. On approaching them, Taylor was attacked and killed. The offenders escaped in the patrol vehicle but were later captured and given life sentences.

Those were 'true' life sentences but, for Wilson, there was an end to his jail term. Following his release, Wilson established an IT business as he attempted to carve out a new life for himself. That was not the outcome many had hoped for. In the aftermath of the sentencing in the 1970s, protests took place in George Square in Glasgow, calling for the death penalty to be reintroduced and for Wilson to be executed. Capital punishment had been abolished just two weeks before the murders.

Survivors Campbell and Hyslop, who was forced to retire from the police service on health grounds, were both awarded the George Medal in recognition of their bravery during the Allison Street incident. Barnett and MacKenzie received the Queen's Police Medal posthumously. It was in 2000 that

Hyslop passed away on Islay where he was living by that time. Friends said he had been constantly haunted by the events of that fateful day in 1969.

The biggest question for all those who had their lives shattered by the Allison Street horrors was: why did it have to happen? Why did a once-proud policeman turn to such murderous actions?

Wilson, interviewed by the *The Herald* in 1994, answered that when he said: 'Quite simply it was the temptation of easy money – greed and temptation. The message is clear: if I wasn't involved in crime there would have been no weapons and no weapons would have meant no murders. When you commit a crime you never think it will go wrong. You want to take the shortcut – you don't intend the catastrophe.' He added: 'They say "you are doing a life sentence and you are lucky if you get out" and they are right. I live in the real world – accept that I will be lucky ever to be freed. Life is simpler in prison ... What I am concerned with is the price of peanut butter in the canteen – that is what we talk about now.'

Despite his own clear reservations, Wilson was, indeed, allowed to walk free. It was a low-key event, a far cry from the hugely high-profile court case which led to his incarceration.

Representing Wilson at the High Court in 1970, Nicholas Fairbairn talked about debt and the 'fantasy' it created, in the minds of those who were in its clutches, that 'one visit to Aladdin's Cave would result in the terrible burden being gone forever'. That was not the case for Wilson for whom one raid led to another and to horrendous consequences.

The chain of events over his lifetime had taken Wilson down a dangerous path. He was just a toddler when his father died in a shooting accident but his mother, a dance teacher, was determined not to let those tragic early years impact on his upbringing. She remarried and ensured her son had the best possible education, enrolling him in the independent Glasgow Academy. It had an excellent reputation in the city and lists among its former pupils such political beacons as Donald Dewar and Jackson Carlaw, leading figures from the world of media, including BBC founder John Reith, and sporting stars, including rugby great John Beattie. Discipline was an important part of school life and opportunities stretched out in front of those who capitalised on all that was on offer.

Wilson was said to have been a model pupil at the school – a popular rugby-playing boy with big plans for the future. The 6ft 3in figure completed his National Service with an unblemished record and was similarly successful during his time as a policeman in his home city, earning commendations for his commitment during a decade in the force. Frustration at a lack of promotion prospects made him decide to turn his back on a life in uniform and, instead, he set up in business with a greengrocer's shop, known as 'The Orchard', at 1403 Cathcart Road in Mount Florida. The harsh realities of self-employment quickly hit home and, when the enterprise hit rocky times, Wilson, 31 at the time, turned to crime. He was experienced in that world – albeit on the law enforcement side of the fence – and knew he could not act alone.

That is where John Sim, just 22 years old and, like Wilson, a former policeman, came into the equation, along with 31-year-old, Paisley-based mechanic Ian Donaldson. The fourth link in the chain was Archibald McGeachie, who had worked at The Orchard before becoming a partner in the enterprise. The quartet's friendship was strong and Wilson is said to have been quite nonchalant when he first floated the idea of robbing a bank to the rest of the group. The plan quickly gathered pace and it crossed the point of no return in July 1969 at Williamwood.

The unsolved element of the Wilson gang's crimes is what happened to McGeachie. He is known to have received in the region of £4,000 after serving as the getaway driver for the initial raid. The four friends went into partnership in business on the back of their criminal proceeds, establishing the Clydesdale Service Station on Burnbank Road in Hamilton. The friendship later turned sour, with a fall-out between the men, and McGeachie went his separate way. He is said to have received £1,000 for his stake in the garage business and to have used that money to buy a newsagent's shop at 53 Allison Street.

The group remained apart until 22 December 1969, when John Sim was said to have called at McGeachie's shop. It has been claimed that an attempt was made to persuade him to take part in the second bank job which was planned for the following week. The assumption is that he declined that offer but what happened thereafter is unclear. McGeachie was last seen on 23 December at 10.30 p.m., talking to an unknown man. Then he was gone, carrying £60 in cash and a bankbook. He held £350 in two bank accounts but not a penny was touched from that day on.

His family had to turn to the legal world for some form of closure, with the Court of Session ruling in March 1972 that McGeachie was dead. The case brought evidence from detectives who had investigated his disappearance as well as a host of other witnesses, with much of the narrative heard in private to avoid incriminating those who appeared on the stand. It was revealed that the garage McGeachie had once been a partner in was searched by police after he had vanished and a discarded spade had been found lying in the workshop's greasing bay. Although there were traces of blood on the handle and mud and cement on the blade, there was no definitive evidence to support the assertion from McGeachie's family that he had met a violent death.

After he had been declared dead, the newsagent's family took the case to the Criminal Injuries Board in the hope of obtaining an official verdict that he had been murdered. Widespread speculation in Glasgow suggested he had been murdered and had been buried in either the concrete pillars of the Kingston Bridge or the foundations of the M74 during construction. His father told reporters at the time: 'I know Archie was murdered and I have a good idea who did it. From what I understand, the body is almost certain to be under the bridge foundations. The reason we are taking this to the Criminal Injuries Board is that we want the killers of our son to be brought to justice. If they find that my son died by criminal action, we will have something to go on.'

Work on the bridge had begun in 1967 and concluded three

years later. In the interim there were repeated tales of bodies being disposed of in the fabric of the concrete structure. It was said to have been a method used by henchmen of the notorious Glasgow godfather Arthur Thompson. The pillars were eventually broken up in 1999, during reconstruction work, but no reports of any grisly discoveries were made.

The family of McGeachie never did get an answer as to what had happened. In contrast, those related to the murdered policemen knew exactly how their loved ones had been killed – something which in no way eased the pain.

In 2009, widow June MacKenzie spoke for the first time about her sorrow. She told journalists: 'It took me a decade to come to after the incident. It is something you do not get over. It sucked the life out of me and it takes a long time to get going.' She had been serving as a WPC in the police force at the time of the death of her husband but stepped away from that life shortly afterwards and carved out a new career as a PA. June added, 'In those days, there was no counselling or psychological help. There is still a blank piece in my mind.'

She made those comments in advance of a memorial service staged to mark the 40th anniversary of the shocking crime. It had been organised by the Glasgow Police Heritage Society and was held at the city's Linn Crematorium. The society's curator said the deaths made it 'one of the darkest days in the history of the Glasgow Police'.

The wives of Edward Barnett and Angus MacKenzie laid a wreath at the men's graves, which are side by side. Many former colleagues of the two murdered officers also attended. The brave men who sacrificed their lives in their quest to make Glasgow a safer city will never be forgotten.

13

Tricks of the Trade

As the heavy goods vehicle trundled away from Prestwick Airport's cargo area in the early hours of a cool April day, there was no hint of what lay ahead. It picked its way away from the yard and onto the open road with only the occasional flicker of lights from passing cars to light up the gloom and shine a spotlight on the Iveco truck as it motored through the Ayrshire countryside.

The unremarkable vehicle, an ageing curtain-sided lorry, gave nothing away from the outside – certainly not to the untrained eye. But inside its seven-tonne load area was a precious cargo that the driver knew all too well he had to take particular care of. It was not cash or gold, not antiquities or art. Instead, the £500,000 consignment was made up entirely of computer disk drives. It was 2002 and Scotland was playing its part in the post-millennium advances in technology. The parts loaded on the truck had been ordered by Seagate, a US technology firm with a manufacturing base in Irvine. That factory was a 10-mile drive from Prestwick – less than 20 minutes even at a conservative pace. It was a route that was familiar to the delivery network feeding Seagate's operation. During the week in question, the load had arrived on a cargo flight from Singapore and, after being processed by customs officials, had been moved to a storage warehouse ready for collection.

From there, they were to be moved on to the company's plant at Irvine, where a range of internal and external hard drives were manufactured and marketed. The US enterprise had first landed on Scottish soil in 1985 when it opened a factory in Livingston, which was later followed by the Irvine expansion. By the time of the Prestwick heist, Livingston had been closed due to a downturn in demand and Irvine remained teetering on the brink. The loss of more than £500,000 of equipment must have done nothing to hearten the California-based management team who were considering the future of the facility and those it operated in locations as far afield as the Far East.

In 2002 it was business as normal, and when the truck arrived at 4.45 a.m. on 1 April, a Monday morning, there was nothing untoward. The driver presented the necessary paperwork and signed on the dotted line to enable his consignment to be shifted into the back of the lorry ready to make what should have been an uneventful trip. With the administration taken care of, he was bid a brisk farewell by the airport security team and sent off along the journey. Little did the Prestwick team realise that the high-value boxes would not make it to their destination as a meticulously planned and audaciously executed heist began to take shape. The alarm was not raised immediately; instead it took a few hours before police were called in and the missing computer kit was reported.

From the very first stagecoach robbery to the modern day, the theft of valuables in transit has been an unfortunate part of British life. Violence, threats and intimidation have been the common denominator – drivers terrorised purely on the basis of the contents of their vehicle. But that is where the Seagate raiders differed from those who had gone before them. There were no weapons used, no force and no commotion. The only tool required was cunning.

Police called to start the search had to begin with a clean sheet – who, what, where, when and how. Those were the blanks to be filled in and, quite quickly, they began to become clear. By the time the Iveco had been driven out of the Prestwick gates, one of the largest heists in Scotland in recent times had already taken place. The driver was not a victim in waiting but the prime protagonist in the elaborate and very contemporary crime. On this occasion, it proved the pen can, indeed, be

mightier than the sword as a convincing fake paper trail was
used to pull off a robbery which brought maximum return for
very minimal fuss.

When the driver turned up at the airport's bonded freight
warehouse that morning, he came armed not with a gun or
a knife but with a docket entitling him to collect the consignment of computer parts. It was a very good imitation, clearly
put together with knowledge of the real McCoy. The plan was
aided by the sheer volume of cargo movements handled daily
at Prestwick Airport which prides itself on being 'Scotland's
premier dedicated freight airport'. Chiefs at the air hub point
to its location as a major attraction, not least because it serves as
the first mainland point in Europe for transatlantic flights. The
ability to handle large aircraft ensures it is used for everything
from technology shipments to livestock charters, with a significant investment made in guaranteeing freight facilities are
attractive to some of the largest operators in the world. Good
road links to Glasgow and the north of England are another
selling point, whilst fast turnaround of aircraft and processing
of cargo are also hailed in marketing brochures. Crucially, the
airport's 24-hour-a-day, seven-days-per-week opening hours
make it a constant hive of activity and an obvious freight stop
due to the lack of noise restrictions. All of those factors also
left it open to the type of crime suffered by Seagate when the
humble Iveco drove away with its precious goods.

Dressed in work gear, complete with a high-visibility vest,
the driver did nothing to arouse suspicion. He spoke with a
Scottish accent, presented his documentation and patiently
waited for the all clear to load up his truck. The vehicle itself
was not distinctive. A light-coloured cab with blue trim were
the only features to make a lasting impression on the gatehouse
staff who watched it disappear into the distance that morning.
A broken rear light and the number two on one of the doors
were other marks noted at the time.

The lorry pulled away from the airport and could have been
hundreds of miles away by the time the alarm was eventually
raised. The police were only notified after the horrible truth

dawned on the cargo team at Prestwick when Seagate, the rightful owners of the shipment, arrived at the gatehouse to collect their equipment. The documentation was checked and double-checked and the truth became clear.

Although the fake driver, his face partially hidden by a cap pulled down over his brow, had acted alone for the early morning pick-up, detectives were quick to make the assessment that the operation was the brainchild of a highly organised criminal gang. The assumption was the driver was part of the conspiracy but the alternative viewpoint was that he could have been merely a pawn in the process – believing he was collecting a genuine load. If that was the case, he certainly didn't come forward to volunteer information on his part in the theft. Instead, it was left to Seagate to offer a £30,000 reward in the hope of enticing information from those who held the key to solving the case.

As well as reaching out to those who may have had an involvement on the periphery of the scheme or at least knowledge of it through the criminal jungle drums, the company was also hoping to touch a nerve with those providing another link in the chain – potential buyers of the equipment. It was a specialist shipment and a large one at that, so it was not going to be disposed of through the thief's traditional network of barroom bartering and backstreet deals. This would need to find a more expert home – someone involved in either manufacturing or large-scale wholesaling of technology products. With the publicity attracted by the raid Scotland would probably be too close to home, but disposing of it overseas would mean a risky export trail. The natural conclusion was that England would be the likely market and that is where police resources were concentrated, as well as scrutinising the scene and methods used.

The Prestwick incident was not the first breach of airport security on British soil that year. Just two months earlier, raiders had escaped with $4.2 million from a British Airways security van at Heathrow. A month before the Scottish robbery, Heathrow had again been a target when $2.24 million had been taken after it landed on a South African Airways flight. The small consolation at Prestwick was that the computer parts had been stolen once they had been taken 'landside'. From a security perspective, the London thefts had been more concerning since they had occurred on what should have been sacrosanct 'airside' land. Still, an immediate security review was ordered by bosses at the Ayrshire airport, as they came to terms with what had happened on their watch.

Stuart Sinclair, airport freight director at the time, faced the music as media interest grew. He told journalists: 'Some freight was taken erroneously. We are awaiting the result of the investigation. Some very calculating and clever thieves appear to have taken the cargo. Our people acted in a normal manner of distributing the freight once it had cleared customs. The thieves produced documents to overcome our systems. We view an incident like this as very, very serious.

'This appeared to be a normal transaction when someone turned up with forged documents. We went through the processes of issuing a release note for them to collect the freight from our warehouse, only to discover what had happened when the real documents turned up hours later. We will review security to see where there are perhaps any loopholes, but at this moment in time it would be very hard to see how this could have been avoided.'

It was described by investigating officers as 'a well-organised, well-executed crime' and it was made clear that the culprits knew exactly what they had come for and how to get away with it. And, having hit on a winning formula, there was little incentive for them to give up. Three months later, a similar charade was played out on the opposite side of the country. This time, it was at Grangemouth docks and the stock of choice was more high proof than high tech – with Absolut vodka spirited away from the harbour by a smooth-talking conman in an articulated lorry. The cases were worth £200,000 and, once again, were released by staff at the cargo base when the driver produced what appeared to be authentic documents. The trailer was loaded up and the contents driven away without so much as a flicker of concern – it was a confident and well-rehearsed routine.

Just as at Prestwick months earlier, the crew responsible relied upon the busy nature of the port to enable them to blend into the background. Grangemouth, the country's largest container port and within easy reach of Edinburgh and Glasgow, handles around 9 million tonnes of cargo every year – equating to 150,000 containers annually. That represents 150,000 container loads which require to be hauled away from the area, ensuring the movement of a lorryload of vodka was of little significance. It flew under the radar, particularly given the apparent presence of all necessary documentation.

With 500,000 sq. ft of warehouse accommodation, spread across 365 acres, Grangemouth is a huge complex and the gang were able to motor away with no disruption – and with £200,000 worth of easily saleable alcohol safely tucked away and ready to flood Britain's booming black market. That underground trade was picking up at the turn of the millennium, as aggressive taxation began to bite. Estimates using official HMRC data provide an eye-watering snapshot of the level of the black market in the UK – making the Grangemouth vodka heist look like a small drop in the ocean of illicit beer and spirits washing around Britain.

In 2012, the TaxPayers' Alliance (TPA), a group that campaigns for the lowering of taxes and public spending, compiled a comprehensive rundown of the market and came up with the assessment that £28.5 billion of tax revenue had been lost through the illegal sale of spirits, beer, cigarettes, tobacco and diesel between 2005 and 2010 alone. The alliance argued that taxing those goods in a punitive manner would only exacerbate the problem and also warned against the minimum pricing strategy for alcohol which was at that stage looming on the horizon. It prompted the then TPA director Matthew Sinclair to say: 'High taxes also create fat profits for criminals. With new tax hikes, and proposals for a minimum price on alcohol, the Chancellor runs the risk of making that black market even more profitable. The revenue lost to the illicit trade could fund a small but welcome tax cut for millions of families, but instead it's lining the pockets of those selling dodgy diesel, tobacco and booze. The Government need to give struggling taxpayers a better deal and squeeze the smugglers.'

It wasn't just the smugglers who were fuelling the black market – thieves were also at the centre of the trade. By the time the Grangemouth theft was discovered, there was every chance the bottles of vodka were already being distributed as it was not until days after they had been taken that the facts became clear and police were once again called in to investigate what was starting to become a trend north of the Border.

Grangemouth was the latest, Prestwick had been the previous and there had also been two earlier incidents of note. Those occurred early in 2002 – one in Ayrshire when a trailer containing £750,000 of computer equipment was stolen from an industrial estate and the other in Bridgton, Glasgow, when a similar batch, this time worth £250,000, was removed unlawfully. On each occasion, forged paperwork was used to gain easy access and allow the perpetrators to make good their escape without being challenged.

Following the successful vodka heist, Detective Sergeant Pat Scroggie of Central Scotland Police stated, 'One positive line of inquiry is in England where the stuff appears to be getting sold. It is possible one gang may be responsible as, when they find a fraud that works, they try it again and again.'

In June 2005, there was another attack at Prestwick although it was different in nature. A three-man gang armed with knives threatened a member of staff and exited with £275,000 worth of computer gear. The employee was left badly shaken but uninjured. The somewhat inconvenient factor of the timing of the theft was that it came just weeks before the world's leaders were due to fly in to Scotland, many through Prestwick, for the G8 summit at Gleneagles. Airport bosses were forced to defend their security procedures and policies. They vowed to improve systems to protect the warehouse complex. The difficulty was that the freight area was a busy part of the airport, with a constant flow of heavy goods vehicles and vans coming and going day and night. It made the task of controlling and monitoring each movement challenging, especially in the face of increasingly determined attempts to get the better of the security staff. In truth, those robberies had no bearing on the G8 preparations – the small matter of 3,000 police officers enlisted to guard Prestwick's perimeter made sure of that.

In 2004, the investigation into the 2002 Prestwick heist wended its way to court when two notorious figures joined nine fellow-accused in the dock. Martin Bowers and his brother Tony were, up to that point, best known for their role at the heart of British boxing. They managed the renowned Peacock Gym in London and served as promoters. Lennox Lewis, Prince Naseem Hamed and many other household names had used their Canning Town gym as a training base and some gym users were even cast in the gangster film *Snatch* by Guy Ritchie. Then the siblings became infamous for very different reasons as they faced up to charges that they were part of a gang behind a flurry of robberies and hijackings at airports and ports on both sides of the border. These included the £1.1-million raid of HSBC cash at Gatwick in March 2004 when robbers posed as Brinks Mat guards to get to the bank's stored money. Bags of cash being deposited from Gibraltar were the target for that airport raid. The other end of the spectrum was the Grangemouth docks robbery.

It transpired police had spent nine months filming the Peacock gym, which served as headquarters for the alleged enterprise. The gym also became the centre of attention for the media, hungry for the celebrity aspect of the court case. A smattering of well-known names peppered the story and this ensured maximum exposure for the trial. Naturally, the scale of the crime also had an influence on the pick-up by newspapers and broadcasters but the personalities involved were the driving force.

When Tony, Martin and the third Bowers brother, Paul, were jailed, it was revealed in court that Gatwick was viewed as 'the big one' by the gang. The series of raids had been planned to raise funds to save their struggling gym on the back of a huge rent hike. They had vowed to stick to a no-weapons, no-violence policy. Their reward was not a happily-ever-after scenario – Tony was jailed for twelve and a half years, Martin for seven years and Paul for six. Eight accomplices were also jailed after admitting their role. They had, between the three of them, admitted charges of conspiracy to steal and conspiracy to obtain by deception and handle stolen goods between August 2002 and May 2003. Prosecutor Timothy Barnes QC revealed insiders were recruited to 'create an array of bogus documents and false identities' in order to target valuable consignments arriving at the airports and docks. Gary Kibbey, of the Met's Serious Crime Squad, said the gang had committed 'organised crime on a massive scale'.

As an aside, it is worth noting that lorry crime did not end with the conclusion of the Bowers court case. In the summer of 2013, a trailer containing £300,000 worth of wine was whipped away from a yard in Uddingston, Lanarkshire, by thieves who arrived with their own lorry cab to haul the valuable freight.

For police those thefts marked a great challenge to investigate but, with the absence of weapons and violence, were far more palatable than some of the vicious and even deadly attacks of the past. With no arms involved, the Prestwick and Grangemouth incidents demonstrated the potential profits on offer for those who carried out such robberies. Computer parts and alcohol were relatively new targets for the underworld but a high-profile case in Perth underlined the fact that more familiar treasures remained in demand. In 2009, a patient and well-organised gang struck in the centre of the city to pull off what was, at the time, Scotland's biggest-ever jewellery theft. Again, there was no hint of violence or sense of drama – instead, sleight of hand was the order of the day.

The setting for the lightning-quick raid was unusual, given the high value of the goods. In a matter of seconds, thieves had escaped with jewellery worth £1 million on the High Street when they snatched a holdall from a travelling salesman as he took a break from his work to browse in an Oxfam charity store. The shop, on Perth's South Street, became the centre of attention for one of the country's biggest criminal investigations as detectives and uniformed officers swarmed around the area in the aftermath of the sneak theft.

The shell-shocked 62-year-old salesman was left to break the news to his employers, a leading jewel merchant based in the trade's heartland of Hatton Garden in London. It was a family-run firm, making the loss of the haul of precious diamond rings, bracelets and necklaces all the more devastating.

Hatton Garden's jewellery quarter is a sight to behold, with gem merchants and jewellers at every turn. The success of the area is built upon the experience of the craftsmen and specialists who have been operating for generations, importing precious stones and manufacturing exquisite pieces. Quantity and quality are bywords and competition is fierce. Behind every fine merchant is an active sales force, dedicated to selling the wares to jewellers far and wide. It was during one of those trade missions to Scotland that one Hatton Garden firm came a cropper and their lax security was cruelly exposed.

The salesman had been carrying a range of jewellery in a blue canvas sports bag, desperate not to draw attention to his high-value goods, as he visited a stockist in Perth. He had clearly been carefully watched by the gang, who followed him to the Oxfam outlet and struck when his attention had momentarily switched away from the bag. Unlike cash-carrying security teams, there was no high-tech system in place to make life difficult for the assailants – undoubtedly a factor in their choice of target. The victim was browsing the second-hand book section of the shop and his tome of choice would prove to be the most expensive he is ever likely to read. The wholesale value of the stock was put at £600,000, translating to a seven-figure sum when priced for the retail market. He had placed the bag on the floor as he leafed through the books on the shelves and that proved to be long enough for the gang to set to work.

Police believed the gang may have been a well-travelled group which had struck at various points across Europe, leading the Tayside force to open discussions with counterparts throughout Britain and on the Continent as they stepped up their investigations. Attention focused on three individuals who had been seen in and around the Oxfam shop on the day of the incident. It is believed they were travelling in an ageing dark-coloured BMW which was also seen in the area at the time. It was reported that the car had been tailing the salesman for 'some time', its occupants clearly waiting for an opportune moment to strike and deciding that they had found their perfect window.

The description of the first suspect was particularly distinctive – with officers seeking information about 'an attractive-looking' woman of 'European appearance' who was seen acting suspiciously in the store shortly before the bag vanished. She was said to be aged between 20 and 25, 5ft 2in in height, slim, with brown wavy hair and, crucially, it was thought she had also been in the Perth jewellers that the salesman had visited that day. Two men were witnessed getting into the BMW with the woman, driving off at speed in the direction of Tay Street and presumably leaving Perth by one of the fast links heading north and south provided by the A90 dual carriageway. They had negotiated the busy streets of the bustling city without being apprehended and there were only a few eyewitness statements to help guide the investigation. The first man was described as being of dark complexion with 'a European appearance'. He was 5ft 9in in height and had thinning grey hair. His sidekick was said to be of Asian appearance, in the region of 6ft with thick dark hair.

A week after the incident, police returned to the scene and desperately attempted to jog memories and spur the Perth public to come forward with information. Mike Pirie, the detective charged with leading the probe, said at the time: 'We are studying hours of public and private CCTV coverage to try and identify any suspicious activity in the area that could assist in tracing those responsible. Our officers are also working closely with colleagues in other force areas to see if they can assist our enquiries. In addition, we have had a good response from members of the public who have contacted us to offer valuable details.'

Perth's Sleepy Hollow image was all of a sudden blown out of the water as the thriving city with its rural charm and well-to-do reputation found itself at the centre of a major criminal probe. Residents found themselves being stopped in the street to answer questions from reporters and the business community was also being pushed to give their input. Some were comfortable in the spotlight but most chose to shy away. Whatever approach was taken, there was no escaping the fact that their town was the centre of attention – it was Perth's 15 minutes of fame.

The unfortunate victim was named by some newspapers. A South African national, his job had taken him to Scotland from his base in London. He did not return to England from his business trip with happy memories. Understandably, he was said to have been left deeply distressed by the incident – the definite low point in career said to have spanned four decades. He had been a regular visitor to Perth, and on his ill-fated trip had kept an appointment at Timothy Hardie, a jewellery store on St Johns Street. Established in 1981, it is an outlet well known for its specialism in antique gems and boasts the largest selection of Victorian and Edwardian pieces in the country. With some very well known clients, including golfer Colin Montgomerie, it was regarded as having great potential for the London merchants with high-end products to sell.

The store's owner said at the time, 'I am shocked that this could have happened. You don't expect something like this to happen in the Fair City of Perth. But it is obvious from what the police are saying that it was planned.'

As well as trawling through hours of CCTV footage, police also took to the streets to conduct door-to-door inquiries in the commercial heart of the city. Businesses and householders were asked to provide any information they felt relevant. The firm which had suffered the loss also offered a £50,000 reward for information leading to the return of the contents of the bag and specialist jewellery publications were used to circulate details of the missing items. Yet, to date, the mystery of the Oxfam heist remains unsolved and hundreds of thousands of pounds worth of breathtaking jewellery remains undiscovered, presumably finding its way, piece by piece, into the hands of unsuspecting buyers. Behind every stone is a story and, in the case of that batch, it was a more extraordinary tale than most.

14

The Art of the Heist

With alarm bells ringing, pulses racing, hearts thumping and voices raised, the peace and tranquillity of the Dumfriesshire countryside was shattered. What the commotion signified was the most significant art heist in the history of Scotland and, to this day, the men responsible remain at large and the mystery of the painting known as *The Madonna of the Yarnwinder* is unsolved.

It was on 27 August 2003 that Drumlanrig Castle's place in history changed forever. Once best known as the seat of the Duke of Buccleuch, in an instant, it became notorious as the scene of a crime which sent shockwaves reverberating around the world. The painting was said to be worth anything up to £50 million, but to the family from whom it had been wrenched away it was utterly priceless.

The scenic castle, a popular summer attraction, had just opened for another day. Tour guide Alison Russell, just 25 years old at the time, was doing the job she loved when her life was turned upside down. As she welcomed guests to the stunning surroundings at 11 a.m. on a Wednesday morning, it turned out two of the day's visitors were not out for an innocent sightseeing excursion. Instead, they were preparing for a terrifying attack on the staff and property at Drumlanrig.

As Russell went about her work, one of the men approached her from behind and menacingly placed his hand over her mouth. He was calm and composed, ordering the terrified guide to get down on the floor. She was told if she did not follow orders she would be killed. The assailants, one armed with an axe, proceeded to carefully remove a painting from the spot where it took pride of place. That painting was *The Madonna of the Yarnwinder*, by Leonardo da Vinci. Alarms were triggered as soon as the frame was pulled from the wall, causing staff from other areas of the castle to hurry to the Staircase Gallery to find out what was happening. At least one of those on duty that day was in her 70s and the sight of the axe-wielding raider understandably caused her great distress.

Unperturbed by being centre of attention, the culprits made their escape through a nearby window and made a run for it. Unbeknown to them, gardener John Chrystie was working in the castle grounds near to where they appeared, clutching the distinctive painting, and the brave estate worker gave chase. Chrystie had recognised the precious heirloom being carried by one of the men and knew how much it meant to his employers. Without a second thought, the 50-year-old set off in pursuit of the group but he was forced to back off when one produced the axe and warned him off continuing on their trail. Regardless of the value of the art, the clear and violent threat was a reminder of the potential high price that would be paid by anyone who crossed what was clearly a ruthless and efficient gang.

The men, with the da Vinci safely in their possession, jumped into an ageing white Volkswagen Golf GTI and sped off into the Dumfriesshire countryside, negotiating the winding rural roads as they bulleted away from the castle on what transpired was a well-rehearsed and well-thought-out exit route. Witnesses saw the getaway car on the road between Thornhill and the Durisdeer road shortly afterwards but, thereafter, lost sight of it. It was believed that there were four men in the car, presumably including two accomplices of the pair who had carried out the raid itself.

CCTV at the castle captured images of the men at the scene. The first was thought to be in his early 40s, 5ft 10in tall with a slim build. He wore brown shoes, cream trousers, a cream T-shirt, brown nubuck leather jacket, a brown baseball cap and round-framed glasses. The other was said to be in his late 40s, roughly the same height and build, and wore black trousers, black shoes, a cream long-sleeved shirt, a sleeveless, taupe safari-type jacket and a light cream wide-brimmed hat. Their distinctive appearance raised two possibilities. Either the duo had opted to dress in a manner which they felt fitted in with the stately home surroundings or they had attempted to disguise themselves from the cameras they knew would be monitoring their movements. There is something peculiar about watching the raiders making their escape, looking more like a group out for a high tea than pulling off a multi-million-pound heist. It was more straw boater than balaclava.

The white Golf they had made their rapid retreat in, an able driving machine despite its vintage, was discovered abandoned in a forest just a short drive from the castle. Only a couple of miles away and shielded by the woodland, the gang are believed to have transferred into a black BMW and set off from the heart of the investigation and to safety. It was quickly suspected that the thieves then used that car to escape to Mitchellslacks in the Forest of Ae, near Dumfries. With no further sightings of the car after this, the trail ran cold. Such meticulous arrangements demonstrated the planning and intricacy of their blueprint for a huge crime.

Back at the castle, distressed staff had summoned police from the Dumfries and Galloway Constabulary. It was Scotland's smallest police force, in the days before the centralised Police Scotland came to pass, but they now faced one of the country's most high-profile cases. However, some of the officers had great experience in the most testing of circumstances, having dealt with the horrors of the Lockerbie disaster.

The Drumlanrig heist was in no way comparable to that atrocity but it did serve to put the area back under intense scrutiny for reasons everyone involved would rather have avoided. With the fear that the painting would be quickly shipped overseas, the immediate response was to alert Interpol. Ports, rail terminals and airports were all put on high alert and made aware of the incident.

The Madonna of the Yarnwinder was believed to date back to 1501. It had been created for Florimond Robertet, secretary to the King of France, and depicts Jesus sitting on the Virgin

Mary's lap, holding her yarnwinder. Shaped like a cross, the yarnwinder is said to anticipate Jesus's crucifixion. The painting had been bought in the 18th century in Italy by the third Duke of Buccleuch and taken back to Scotland to its new home.

The Earl of Dalkeith, the son of the Duke of Buccleuch, said at the time of the theft:

> This is a treasure that has been in my family for more than 250 years. It's the most beautiful work of art by one of the greatest painters in the world. It is a work of such peace and beauty and the thought of it being sort of torn away from us like this is very sad indeed. Thousands of people have come over the years to see it. It's not been shut away and just enjoyed by us.

The significance of the stolen painting could not be over-stated. It was described in some quarters as akin to the Mona Lisa being taken. The masterpiece formed part of an incredible art collection assembled by the Duke of Buccleuch, who in 2003 was ranked just outside of the top 50 wealthiest people in Britain. His 253,000-acre estate was one of his prime assets but the prized £405-million art collection was another. It featured paintings by Rembrandt, Gainsborough and Holbein to name but a few that would be instantly recognisable to any art lover. Many of those works were made available for public viewing, with the treasured da Vinci piece hanging in the hall of the castle as a centrepiece to the collection.

As the dust settled on the heartbreaking theft, the pain felt by the Buccleuch family became clear. Charles Lister, who managed Drumlanrig Castle, said his employers considered they were simply custodians of the revered piece or art. He said: 'The family do obviously try to remain optimistic about the return of the painting. So, we're looking forward to it coming back as soon as possible. It would be a tragedy if anything happened to it. Not only is it a treasure to the family themselves, but obviously to the thousands of people who have come and seen it in the past. The family likes to display these things to the public. It could have been locked away but His Grace felt he should show it to the people so they could enjoy it themselves.'

The isolated Scottish castle had been exposed as an easy target. Security improvements were made following the raid – not just at Drumlanrig but also by those responsible for similar collections at other historic properties – but ultimately there was an acceptance that little could be done when faced with grim and determined criminals if public access was to be preserved. Experts argued that a daytime raid whilst the castle was open was far more likely to succeed than one under the cover of darkness when doors were bolted shut and intruder alarms activated.

The castle dates back to the second half of the 1600s, having been built on an existing country estate. Today the estate, with its farming and forestry functions, is big business and the tourism element is part of the mix. There are clear and obvious risks in inviting the public, but those were deemed worth taking in order to share the historic home with visitors to the estate. It is hugely popular with tourists from at home and abroad, with its imposing facade making an immediate impact. Overlooking the stunning Nith Valley, it has been dubbed the Pink Palace. It offers guided tours and numerous outdoor activities. The Scottish Cycle Museum is also housed within the grounds, marking local blacksmith Kirkpatrick Macmillan's invention of the bicycle.

What is certain is that the theft was not a passing opportunistic effort. Drumlanrig is a very difficult location to simply stumble across. It sits 61 miles and, more significantly, more than an hour and a half by road from Glasgow. Similarly, it is 63 miles and close to two hours from Edinburgh. Assuming the culprits may have travelled from across the border, Manchester, for example, is fully 171 miles and more than a three-hour car journey away. The gang responsible did not pick this location for its ease of access but because of the treasures it held.

The raid shook the family to the core and the castle's season, already drawing to a close when the painting was snatched, was brought to a premature end. As the Buccleuch family took stock, the art world had its say on the audacious theft.

Edinburgh-based expert Ricky Demarco said the case was 'the most terrifying madness' and added: 'Whoever has it now in their possession is doomed to look after it in secrecy. They are in a state of madness or greed. It is such a beautiful thing, it deserves to be in the hands of people who understand and value it. It is now in the hands of people who put it at risk.'

Quite what would happen to the stolen painting was unclear. Selling such a high-profile item on the open market was practically impossible. Often real paintings would be passed off at auction as high-quality reproductions as a means of avoiding detection and gaining at least a decent return for thieves but this was not going to be an option for the gang involved on this occasion. Every major auction house, gallery and dealer in the world had been made aware of the raid as part of the lock-down effort mounted by officials in charge of the investigation.

A £100,000 reward was quickly put up, with insurers and the family themselves desperate to see the safe return of the item. The insurance firm made a £3-million payment to the Buccleuchs before 2003 had ended but that represented only a fraction of its worth. At that stage, what were described by family representatives as 'complex' insurance issues were revealed. Monetary matters were of secondary interest; the safety of the much-vaunted piece of art was what everyone involved was truly focussing on at a delicate stage of the investigation. One foot wrong could have led to the painting being destroyed or abandoned, making tactics crucial.

In the meantime, police also released CCTV footage which showed the two men who had entered the castle awkwardly attempting to shield their faces from the cameras. Images also showed them getting into the Golf and disappearing into the distance. The car was an important early part of the investigation, with fingertip forensic examinations conducted and the results added to the evidence being gathered. Further CCTV pictures were later released which showed a visit to the castle by two men police were keen to speak to in relation to the raid and, again, one of those men attempted to hide his face when he noticed the watching camera. They had been filmed a week prior to the heist.

Inspector Phil Stewart, of Dumfries and Galloway police, made it clear that he believed the team responsible for the heist had visited the castle previously to scout out their target. Describing the robbery, he said: 'Two men posing as bona fide visitors entered the castle, entered the room where the painting was on display and overpowered a female member of staff. They took the painting and then made good their escape out of the castle.'

In time an e-fit picture of a man who had purchased the Golf two weeks prior to the robbery was created and circulated far and wide but officers admitted their frustration as the investigation failed to bring any immediate progress.

By October 2003 a senior representative from Strathclyde Police had been drafted in to review the progress made to that point, something Dumfries and Galloway chiefs were quick to point out was not unusual in a case of that magnitude. There were, perhaps understandably, whispers locally about the pace with which the investigation was moving but internally there were no concerns. The wheels were in motion but it would take time for the pace to pick up. In November that same year, there was the first significant leap forward.

A seven-year-old dark-green Rover was found in woodland near Drumlanrig. It was believed to have been used by the gang as they plotted the heist, a process which had taken months. It was discovered in the Forest of Ae on 18 November and forensic tests were said to have yielded 'valuable information'. It was the same location at which the thieves were believed to have swapped from their first getaway car, the white Golf, to their second, the black BMW.

A picture of the Rover's movements began to become clear, bringing vital clues to those behind the raid. It had been sold by a garage in October 2002 in Cheshire in north-west England. That legitimate transaction saw the car pass into the hands of a man described as having a Manchester accent and 'greasy, untidy' black hair. Between that moment and the robbery in

Scotland, police were confident it had been used 'extensively' by the gang. Mileage readings pointed to that, as well as pieces of evidence which allowed some of its activity to be plotted.

Whilst the search for those responsible was vital, the hunt for the da Vinci masterpiece was equally important. In 2005 it was placed on the FBI's register of the 10 'most wanted' missing artworks in the world. It sat on the list alongside artefacts looted from the Iraqi National Museum as well as a pair of Van Gogh paintings taken from Amsterdam's Vincent Van Gogh Museum in 2002. *The Scream* and *The Madonna*, by Edvard Munch, also featured following an attack on the Munch Museum in Oslo in 2004 – another daylight robbery. Paintings taken from the Isabella Stewart Gardner Museum in Boston in 1990 – an operation which netted thieves $180-million worth of art including three Rembrandts – were also highlighted. All of those incidents served to shine a light on the scale of the worldwide problem and the fine balance that had to be struck by private collectors and public galleries between allowing the masterpieces to be viewed and ensuring they were protected against callous thefts.

Police in Scotland continued to make sporadic appeals on home soil in an attempt to trace either the offenders or painting but time ran out in 2007 when the Duke of Buccleuch died without his wish of being reunited with his cherished artefact being granted. It was one of the saddest elements of the whole saga.

When he passed away in September 2007, the Duke was 83 years old. A former Conservative MP, he had used a wheelchair following a horse-riding accident in the 1970s but remained an active figure in the community and business world. At the time of his death, he was believed to have been Britain's largest private landowner, with his personal wealth estimated at £85 million. He had been educated at Eton and then Oxford before becoming director of the Buccleuch Estates in 1949. He went on to serve as a Tory councillor before being voted in as MP for Edinburgh North.

Then, the following month, an incredible turn of events gripped a nation which had pushed the Drumlanrig heist to the back of its collective mind. *The Madonna of the Yarnwinder* had been recovered, intact and undamaged. Art lovers the length and breadth of the country breathed a sigh of relief and waited for details on the staggering find. Thursday, 4 October 2007 proved to be a day of high drama. Acting on intelligence, representatives from four crime-fighting organisations stormed a mid-morning meeting between five people in Glasgow city centre and recovered the painting at the scene. It was whisked away to be formally identified by experts. More than 60 officers had been involved in searches of properties in Lancashire and Scotland that culminated in the raid – not on a backstreet hide-out or a dingy warehouse but, rather, on the offices of solicitors HBJ Gateley Wareing in West Regent Street in Glasgow.

As a result of that intensive activity four men were arrested and subsequently appeared at Dumfries Sheriff Court. No details were revealed at the time but the rumour sweeping the city was that a deal relating to the sale of the painting was in the process of being struck when police rudely interrupted. A fifth man was later arrested in the Glasgow suburb of Bearsden and, in 2008, a sixth man, from Airdrie, joined them. After a slow start, it was an investigation which was gathering great momentum.

Dumfries and Galloway Police led a joint operation with the Scottish Crime and Drug Enforcement Agency (SCDEA), Serious Organised Crime Agency (SOCA) and Strathclyde Police. The partnership appeared to have been effective, certainly in recovering the artwork.

Detective Chief Inspector Mickey Dalgleish, who had been leading the investigation, welcomed the development. He said: 'We are extremely pleased to recover *The Madonna of the Yarnwinder* painting. The recovery of this artwork is down to extensive police enquiries and the combined efforts of several Scottish police forces, the SCDEA and SOCA. For four years police staff have worked tirelessly on the theft and with help from the public we have been able to track down and locate the painting.'

For the new Duke of Buccleuch, who had inherited the title

following his father's death, it was a bittersweet moment. Joy at the return of the heirloom was tempered by deep regret that the man who had held it so dear had not lived long enough to enjoy the moment. The new Duke thanked police for their efforts, saying: 'The tenacity they have shown in pursuing the case for four years has been remarkable and we pay tribute to the skill and courage clearly demonstrated by this very satisfactory outcome.

'Our pleasure is inevitably tinged by sadness that my father, who died just a month ago, should not have lived to see the safe return of this wonderful work of art. It is worth remembering that the Leonardo was on public display at the time, as it had been at his instigation, for nearly three decades. He was dismayed that not only he and his family, but the wider public, would be denied the chance of drawing pleasure from it.

'It appears superficially to be in remarkably good condition but the National Gallery of Scotland has kindly agreed that it should go in the near future to its conservation department for closer examination. Although it will clearly require much thought and preparation, I should say that we are determined that the painting should once again go on public view to be enjoyed by many thousands who we hope will come back to see it in its home at Drumlanrig.'

In fact, it was at the National Gallery in Edinburgh that the painting was next displayed to the public. In December 2009 it was unveiled in the capital, where it benefited from the intense security protocol and systems in place at the venue. It had been loaned to the gallery by the Buccleuch family and went on to feature at the National Gallery in London, one of nine da Vinci masterpieces displayed as part of a special exhibition. Only 15 da Vinci paintings are thought to have survived worldwide.

The Duke later admitted: 'It was hugely emotionally important for all of us in the family, but I think for my father in particular, who felt most keenly its loss. It was clear to anyone who knew him that he was deeply upset by the loss and by the lack of any progress in recovering the painting.'

Those responsible for the theft have never been brought to justice. The only court action in relation to the heist came in March 2010 when five of the six men arrested around the time the painting was recovered stood trial at the High Court in Edinburgh.

Marshall Ronald, 53, Robert Graham, 57, and John Doyle, 61, all from Lancashire, Calum Jones, 45, of Renfrewshire, and David Boyce, 63, of Lanarkshire all denied conspiring to extort £4.25 million and an alternative charge of attempted extortion. They were accused of attempting to get members of the Duke of Buccleuch's family and their insurers to pay for the safe return of the painting. At no stage were they implicated in being involved in the theft of the artwork. At the end of a seven-week trial, all five walked free from court. The case was found not proven against Marshall Ronald, Robert Graham and John Doyle whilst Glasgow solicitors Calum Jones and David Boyce were found not guilty. It had taken the jury eight hours to reach their verdict – one which prosecutors and police had to accept at the end of a long effort to bring the case to court.

During the trial details of an undercover police operation to recover the artwork were revealed. It had been prompted when solicitor Ronald had contacted a loss adjuster and inquired about a potential reward if he could return the painting. He had done so in response to an approach by private investigators Graham and Doyle who said they could track down the painting. After the case, all of the accused welcomed the verdict. Doyle was particularly vocal, insisting the group were entitled to a reward for their part in returning what he described as 'a culturally-significant masterpiece' and he pointed to the fact that neither the police nor insurance company had managed to do that. Doyle added, 'We brought it back and we have been through two-and-a-half years of hell since.'

Graham and Doyle later outlined the intricate detail of the events which brought them before the judge and jury in Edinburgh. It was in October 2007 that they claimed to have 'rescued' the artwork from underworld figures. They checked in at a country house hotel, unwrapped the parcel and took pictures of themselves with the item to ensure they had proof of its existence.

Graham and Doyle ran the Crown Private Investigations agency together and branched out with the creation of a website entitled Stolen Stuff Reunited, providing a vehicle for items to be returned in exchange for a reward or finder's fee. Graham explained, 'It was designed for little things of sentimental value to the people they were taken from but that were of no use to thieves. We never dreamed of something like the da Vinci coming along.'

It was claimed Doyle had been approached in a pub by someone who had information on the painting's whereabouts – the suggestion was that it had come in to the possession of a Liverpool businessman. The pair of private detectives are said to have taken it upon themselves to organise the repatriation and enlisted the help of local solicitor Marshall Ronald, who then brought in a Glasgow legal firm.

Contact was made with who they thought were the loss adjusters dealing with the missing painting and, in October 2007, the duo arranged to collect the painting from go-betweens in a car park in Merseyside. They went on to deliver the painting to the offices of the Glasgow solicitors who were advising them but were greeted by an unexpected welcome, as police flooded in to reclaim the painting. There was no big reward – simply a charge sheet.

The court case did not lead to convictions and, with the raiders still at large, art lovers were left to lament what was seen as an unsatisfactory and open-ended conclusion to police activity around the case of *The Madonna of the Yarnwinder*. It could well be that the full story of an amazing chapter in Scotland's criminal history has yet to be written.

15

An Age-old Problem

What do get when you cross some Masonic chains from
Edinburgh, ancient coins from Perth, rhino heads from Elgin
and an acclaimed painting by the French artist Jean-Baptiste-
Camille Corot and pull them all together? No, not a bad joke
but, rather, a common thread which has run through the world
of crime and punishment for generations.

That thread is one of art and antiquities – commodities
which have attracted those of a less-than-honest persuasion
like moths to a flame, for as long as museums and galleries
have had locks on their doors. And Scotland has been far from
immune to that shadowy world – as the da Vinci theft perfectly
illustrated.

The art loss register, active in Britain since 1991, recorded
in the region of 60,000 missing collectables in the space of its
first 20 years. These staggering statistics were supported by
research published in 2013 which claimed that organised criminal gangs are responsible for thefts of art and antiques totalling
£300 million each year. It is second only to the proceeds of
drug dealing in the criminal league table in Britain – and, most
worryingly of all, police have pointed to the increasing use of
violence in the pursuit of illegally acquiring valuable artefacts.
The Association of Chief Police Officers (ACPO) was behind
the research and members were growing so concerned about
the problem that they produced a detailed strategy in response
to the escalation. Their plan featured a national intelligence
database and an increase in the number of officers allocated to
investigating thefts.

One example was the theft of a rare medieval jug from the Stockwood Discovery Centre in Luton in 2012. It was one of only three known to exist and was valued in the region of £750,000. Known as 'the Wenlok jug', it was recovered and returned to its rightful home, although it had been damaged during the incident. A man arrested in connection with the jug's disappearance was later jailed for handling stolen goods.

Andy Bliss, the chief constable of Hertfordshire and the man charged with leading ACPO's heritage and cultural property crime working group, said: 'Just a single item can be worth many millions of pounds and those sorts of items will appeal to criminals right around the world. They may major in art and antiquities but very often there will be links to money laundering, there'll be links to violence and firearms, and often of course to drugs. Where there's money to be made, organised criminals will move in if we don't stop them.'

Detective Superintendent Adrian Green, involved in investigations across Britain, told the BBC in 2013: 'This is top-level international organised crime and it runs into tens of millions of pounds. What we're seeing is that the value of items is increasing but also the level of violence that they are prepared to use is increasing, which is obviously a major concern to law enforcement. It's robbing our communities of their heritage but it's also putting millions of pounds into the pockets of criminals.'

The grim warnings from leading police officers were noted far and wide. In the spring of 2013 officials at a museum in the north of Scotland were forced to take drastic and regrettable action, removing some of their most treasured artefacts from display in the face of a very real and very serious threat against the traditionally quiet establishment. The Elgin Museum, in Moray, had long given pride of place to two rhinoceros heads – brought back to Scotland as trophies by explorers in the 19th century. What hadn't been appreciated up to that point was just how valuable the horns were. The black market stemmed from demand in China, where they are used in the production of medicines and each horn could be worth a considerable sum.

The remedies are used to treat everything from impotence to headaches and even cancer. The material was also said to be used to make a powerful aphrodisiac. Powdered rhino horn was said to be more valuable than gold by a ratio of 2:1 and, on that basis, it was estimated that the pair of exhibits in Elgin were valued at £400,000. Each kilogram was said to be able to fetch £50,000.

There had been a clutch of thefts on the Continent and intelligence suggested Elgin was on the radar of thieves aiming to service that issue of supply and demand. This led to the difficult decision being taken to remove the heads from display and store them securely behind closed doors at the National Museum of Scotland's facility in Edinburgh. Unlike the national premises, Elgin had only limited security protection and a policy of being safe rather than sorry was adopted on the back of 20 attacks on museums and auction houses in Europe.

Janet Trythall, vice-president of the Moray Society which operates the Elgin Museum, said at the time: 'We were advised to remove the two rhino heads by the National Museum in Edinburgh and our mentors. Unfortunately we had no choice but to remove them from the museum as we didn't want to put our staff, volunteers or visitors at risk from one of these attacks.

'It's one thing to have exhibits stolen and our safe broken into, but to have anyone injured in the process would be devastating. We're gutted to have to lose them, they'll be a huge loss to the museum but after reading the reports from the Museum Association we could clearly tell we couldn't secure these precious items sufficiently.

'In my opinion, there's no way we can have them back. It's not like we don't have security, but it would have been inappropriate to keep the rhino heads, we don't have the resources. We could have replaced the horns with plastic replicas but it's very expensive to do that. Besides, are thieves going to be meticulous? It's possible they might strike first, then only to realise their mistake afterwards. The message we want to get across is that we have no rhino material on our premises any longer.'

The two heads, one of a white rhino and the other from a black one, had been part of the collection at Elgin since 1941. The white rhino was shot in Sudan in 1913 and claimed by the father of Lieutenant Colonel Stuart Menzies from the Arndilly House estate in the Morayshire village of Craigellachie. The black rhino was from Northern Rhodesia. In addition to the rhino heads, the museum also held an 18th-century cup made from rhino horn to the Edinburgh storage area. The late Ming dynasty piece hailed from China.

The decision in Elgin came a year after a gang had attempted to remove a rhino horn from a Norfolk Museum. Janet Trythall added: 'We were obviously concerned that someone might try and steal the rhino heads. There have been reports of many thefts of rhino material from museums over the past couple of years, on the Continent and in England, often involving forced entry while the building has been occupied, and the use of CS gas spray. Many of these thefts have been violent thefts, and we had to think about the safety of our staff and volunteers. The horns are of sufficient value that people are prepared to take desperate measures to steal rhino horns.

'We tried to find alterative solutions. We had installed a panic button at the door in the first instance, but after being con-tacted by a member of the staff from the cultural collections at the National Museums, we decided the exhibits just had to go. It's awful to be dictated by these gangs as to what you are able to display, but we have to be realistic.'

Edinburgh's museums had taken the same step and removed its items from public display, years earlier and Glasgow fol-lowed that lead in 2011 after an audit on security precautions.

Scotland's links to the trade in illicit antiquities may be long established – as the McTear's heist and previous attacks on museums and galleries have proven – but the subject has been given a modern twist and a previously unthinkable air of respectability.

The quartet responsible for that shift in emphasis hail not from an East-end pub or a shadowy underpass but rather from the teak and polish surroundings of the University of

Glasgow. Simon Mackenzie, Neil Brodie, Suzie Thomas and Donna Yates were granted more than £1 million in funding by the European Research Council in 2012 to launch a four-year study into the global trafficking of cultural objects. They set up home at the Scottish Centre for Crime and Justice Research and set about delving into one of the most profitable black market sectors.

One of the facets of the programme was to examine the potential links between what so often is viewed as one of the 'softer' crimes and organised crime as a whole. Simon Mackenzie observed: 'Compared to the trade in narcotics, we know virtually nothing. The narcotics trade has been heavily researched. There are specialist areas within the fields – country experts, modes of regulation. There's been all sorts of research into the people producing drugs, the mechanisms for supply and demand. For people studying cultural heritage traffic, its a good place to start.'

Mackenzie and his colleagues aimed to use their project to paint an accurate picture of the scale of the problem, not just in Scotland but globally.

He added: 'The first largest international market is drugs. The second is arms. Third is everything else – wildlife says it's the third largest, antiquities says it's the third largest, several others also claim to be the third largest. The evidence disappears and nobody has any idea how big it is. Part of our project is to create more accurate sizing statistics.'

Regardless of the true size of the market for stolen antiquities, the University of Glasgow team believe there is little doubt that it represents an issue on a par with crimes perhaps considered 'harder' by popular consensus.

Mackenzie said: 'There is clearly organized crime in the antiquities market, as we conventionally conceive of organized crime. The more interesting question is whether antiquities trafficking is in itself an organized crime. It's not what we would think of as organized crime on its face [sic] because the actors are often quite respectable figures. It seems counter-intuitive to say that museums and auction houses are organized crime.

But look at the definition of organized crime: three or more people operating over a sustained period of time in a serious criminal way. Antiquities trafficking meets that definition. So you can make a technical argument quite easily.

'The more interesting question to ask is: why do we care whether it's organized crime? The policy response to organized crime, the regulatory response, is much greater, more of an international threat. So the distinction can be quite important on a policy basis.

'The reason why organized criminals are involved in the antiquities trade is because it's under-regulated. But you can take the organized criminal out of the antiquities trade and you'll still have looting. It's a story of supply and demand on an international basis. The trade attracts organized criminals, but they don't define the shape of it because it is created and sustained by more conventional trade actors.'

Mackenzie has dismissed the notion that the theft of art and antiquities is in any way victimless, believing preserving items of historical significance is a vital function of modern society. He added: 'It's difficult. The general public is not particularly interested in the context of any particular object dug up in a far-flung corner of the world. And yet, museums and cultural debates are a strong current full of voices who feel very strongly about people's culture and human rights. So in one sense, it's certainly true that sometimes people don't get that broken old pots are important to mankind. But when you elevate that to a greater concern with history and culture and knowledge and civilization, what that means and how we might find our way forward, people do care quite deeply about that. These are fundamentals.'

How the issue is tackled is something the academics do not yet have a definitive answer for, although work is being undertaken to find a solution to that thorny problem. Mackenzie said: 'Most criminologists agree that supply-side interventions are going to be problematic, particularly on their own. The drug trade and prohibition are pretty good examples of trying to control something where there's a high level of demand in a globalized economy. None of these have particularly good records of success.

'Most of the current ideas seems [*sic*] to be about reducing demand or, alternatively, taking an end-to-end type solution – take both ends seriously and start to unwind the economic cultural and social forces underpinning the market. Once you see that, strict legal responses begin to look problematic. It's very difficult for the law to seriously engage with an entrenched, large-scale global trade.

'The nature of regulatory intervention in the cultural heritage market has largely been legal. Mostly its [*sic*] been about UNESCO, passing laws in source countries, prohibition of theft, and passing laws in market countries to prevent purchase. The interesting question for regulation is how do we build up systems around these laws we have.

'Some scholars ... have argued that increasing regulation produces the black-markets – that regulators are culpable for the illicit trade. I've never really bought into that. It's a dead end: if you believe that, what do you do, stand back? You can talk about decriminalizing cannabis use, where the moral limitations are so widely disputed so there's a general debate about whether it should be a crime. But not many people would seriously argue that knowingly stealing cultural property is ok. It's reasonably clear that all sides say it's wrong. Therefore the idea that we should decriminalize it doesn't seem to do much except legitimate illicit stuff. It wouldn't stop the illicit trade. It might make it worse.'

To suggest that all crimes involving antiquities were related to significant gangs would not be accurate. In 2001, a museum attendant was jailed for six months after admitting he had stolen antique coins worth £160,000 from an unlocked safe at the Perth Museum and Art Gallery. They had been sold on to dealers for far less – one of the items alone, a 14th-century coin, was worth £100,000. An audit at the museum pinpointed the missing pieces and an investigation was launched. It was revealed in court that the offender had received just £8,000 for the entire haul as he attempted to raise cash to feed a heroin addiction. Organised crime, this was not.

On a similar theme, in 2012 it became clear that no institution was sacred. It was then that the Masonic organisation's Roman Eagle Lodge on Johnston Terrace in Edinburgh was targeted by a thief who masqueraded as a workman to gain access to a committee room and promptly made off with a set of ceremonial gold chains from a display cabinet. They dated back to the 1920s and were described as 'irreplaceable' by officials at the lodge. In more tangible terms, the precious metal was said to be worth £5,000.

Lodge secretary Harry Wilson told reporters: 'When I walked into the committee room I got the shock of my life. I thought the display cabinet had just fallen off the wall when I saw the blank space. But as I walked over to it I saw the back had been ripped off and the masonic jewels had been taken out. I think I saw the guy but didn't pay any attention to him because we had workmen coming in and out of the building doing up the windows. I thought it was one of the workmen who was bringing materials in. I suspect he has been in the building before either as a visitor or to one of the Burns Suppers which we had in February, because he seemed to know what he wanted and made a beeline for the committee room where the jewels were exhibited. According to CCTV, he was in and out within three and a half minutes. It would be such a shame if they were melted down for the value of their gold – that would be ridiculous.'

Not all items stolen are lost forever. Early in 2011 there was a major breakthrough for officials in charge of Glasgow's collections when three paintings of special significance were recovered. Worth more than £200,000, they were just about to be sold at auction when details were spotted in a catalogue by an eagle-eyed member of staff at the Kelvingrove Art Gallery and Museum. He alerted police and the pieces were quickly seized. *Wooded Landscape*, a painting by Frenchman Jean Baptiste-Camille Corot was due to go under the hammer at the Edinburgh auction house Lyon & Turnbull but was immediately withdrawn when management were alerted to its dubious background.

Investigations revealed that the individual who had put the painting up for sale had already sold a painting by the Scottish artist Samuel John Peploe. It was tracked down to the premises of an innocent art dealer, who had bought it in good faith, and then taken by police to return to its rightful owner. A third piece, entitled *The Infant Christ* and created by Italian Renaissance artist Federico Barocci, was found when police moved in and raided the home of the individual who had put the items up for auction.

All three paintings had disappeared more than a decade earlier but museum chiefs had opted against publicising their absence. A spokesman for Glasgow Life, the organisation which runs the city's galleries and museums, would only say: 'We're very grateful for the work of the police in bringing these paintings home. However, every praise should be reserved for our senior curator whose keen eye illuminated the fact that the stolen Corot was up for auction. Without his wealth of knowledge and expertise, the works may still have been hanging elsewhere. We will continue to work with UK police forces to ensure any stolen item is returned to Glasgow and we are grateful to the galleries who have readily assisted in this matter.'

A further 10 pieces of art, with the combined value said to be potentially in the millions, remained undiscovered. They had vanished from storage at the Kelvingrove, the Museum of Transport and a site in Maryhill during the 1990s, their theft having been discovered following an audit. Among those missing were paintings bearing the signatures of John Constable and the Scottish landscape artist William McTaggart. How they had been spirited away was unclear.

Glasgow's attractions have been regularly in the headlines due to the misdemeanours of a minority. In 2012, a bronze sculptured head valued at £20,000 was whipped away from a display stand at the Kelvingrove. It was removed at 3.45 p.m. on a Sunday afternoon in February but it took fully 45 minutes for the alarm to be raised, when an employee spotted a space where the head should have been. Entitled *Dreaming*, it was created by the late Gerald Laing – an acclaimed British pop artist who had completed the bronze in 1979 and seen it snapped up for display in Glasgow's museums two years later. It weighed a hefty 12.8kg and would not have been easy to manoeuvre away from its first-floor resting place. But it was.

Police had hours of CCTV footage to look through as they set about trying to track down the culprit. At the time, a spokesman for Glasgow Life said: 'This was a deliberate act. Someone has stolen from the people of Glasgow. As with all of our collections, this work belongs to them. We are working with the police and other agencies and would appeal for the safe return of this work of art. Since reopening after refurbishment in 2006, we have welcomed more than nine million visitors to Kelvingrove and had no incidents of work being taken from public view. Thanks to the quick action of staff, we have been able to identify a short timeframe where we believe the bronze was stolen and are in the process of examining CCTV footage from across the museum to identify those responsible.'

The bronze was recovered shortly after it had disappeared, after an anonymous tip-off led to its discovery. It was found close to the gallery in the West end of the city and was undamaged. Detective Constable Ian Thomson, of Strathclyde Police, said: 'We are continuing our inquiries to trace those responsible for the theft of the statue. I would ask that the person who contacted police anonymously last night to get in touch again. I would also like to thank the public for their help in ensuring that this work of art can now be returned to its rightful place, on show to the public.'

That was a happy ending – unlike in the case of more than 600 other items which were registered as 'missing' from Glasgow's city collection at around the same time. They had disappeared over the course of decades and included paintings, sculptures, weapons from Egypt, First World War artefacts and even Roman pieces.

More modern collectables have not been ignored. In summer 2012, two men were arrested after an Edinburgh art dealer was targeted and paintings valued at £16,000 were stolen during a robbery in the dead of night. The price tags were less significant than the signatures which adorned those pieces – with five by the acclaimed artist Peter Howson among the half dozen removed from the Art Mart on the capital's London Road in May that year.

Police had given chase to two men who fled the scene and quickly traced them, as well as the loot. The duo pleaded guilty to the crime but art dealer Douglas Fyfe, the owner of the gallery, voiced concerns that the paintings had been stolen to order. He claimed: 'They were organised. One painting was hidden behind some of the others and couldn't have been seen from outside, so I think someone had been in before to check out the place. I have been there 13 years and it's the first time anything like this has happened. It's very rare, I haven't heard of anything like this at all in Edinburgh or Scotland even.'

The premises had been locked and were also protected by a metal gate secured with two padlocks, but the thieves forced their way in. Fortunately none of the paintings were damaged during the raid or subsequent police chase and the prosecution which followed brought that particular case of somewhat chaotic art theft to a satisfactory conclusion.

Unfortunately, across Britain, tens of thousands of owners have been less fortunate and their treasured items remain nothing more than a statistic on a growing list of missing artworks and antiquities. Missing, presumed stolen.

16

National Emergency

As the cell door slammed shut in Forfar's police station, the mystery surrounding arguably Scotland's greatest heist was drawing to a close. It was 12 April 1951 and officers had the nation's most wanted under lock and key. There was no food, no water sent to the cell – not even a blanket for the evening stay. There was no legal representation, no communication with the outside world. There were, however, frequent checks – just to make sure that there was no escape.

For the police on duty in the Angus town that evening, it was no ordinary assignment. What sat behind the metal bars of their custody area was not a master criminal but instead a lump of solid rock. It was no ordinary rock – it was the Stone of Destiny.

Whilst the recovery of the stone ended a mysterious chapter in law and order on both sides of the border, in truth, the story was just beginning. For decades, the intriguing tale of the circumstances of the audacious raid has captured the imagination and there is no sign of that abating. When the referendum on Scottish independence was proposed and then scheduled for September 2014, it brought the notion of nationalism to the fore and the debate on both sides of the argument raged on. The only thing that is certain is that it is not a new issue, as the theft – or liberation – of the Stone of Destiny proves.

How it came to rest in a Forfar police cell is just one of many facets to a story with layer after layer beneath the surface. It had been driven to the town by Angus County Police, who took possession of the artefact, which is treasured and disputed in

equal measure, after they were summoned to Arbroath Abbey
– where Scotland had signed a declaration to fight for freedom
in 1320. Just before the police arrived, a car had pulled up at
the historic abbey and the three men inside were greeted by
two town councillors, D. A. Gardner and F. W. A. Thornton,
who both had strong links to the Scottish Convention movement. The Convention had been responsible for the Scottish
Covenant – a petition to the Westminster parliament calling
for home rule. First mooted in the 1930s, the push for Scottish
home rule began to gather pace in the post-war years. John
MacCormick, a leading nationalist, oversaw the drawing up
of the Covenant, which was penned in Edinburgh during a
national assembly of the Scottish Convention. The petition
was eventually signed by around two million people – more
than a third of the total population of Scotland at that time. It
was, however, dismissed out of hand by the UK government.
Not surprisingly, those behind the Covenant were outraged by
this reaction.

Councillor Thornton aided the mysterious trio as they carried the heavy stone towards the abbey whilst Gardner was
dispatched to Arbroath's police office to let them know. And
so the media frenzy began. The stone had been draped in the
Saltire as it was slowly paraded up the aisle and laid at the high
altar – the grave of King William the Lion of Scotland. It was
presented to James Wishart, custodian of the abbey, and he
remained by its side until police arrived.

Delivered with the stone were two unsigned letters. One was
addressed to the King and the other to the General Assembly
of the Church of Scotland. The letter to the King read:

Unto his Majesty King George VI, the address of his Majesty's
Scottish subjects who removed the Stone of Destiny from
Westminster Abbey and have since retained it in Scotland,
humbly showeth.

That in their actions they, as loyal subjects, have intended no
indignity or injury to his Majesty or to the Royal Family.

That they have been inspired in all they have done by their

deep love of his Majesty's realm of Scotland and by their desire to compel the attention of his Majesty's Minister to the widely expressed demand of Scottish people for a measure of self-government.

That in removing the Stone of Destiny they were restoring to the people of Scotland the most ancient and most honourable part of the Scottish regalia, which for many centuries was venerated as the palladium of their liberty and which in 1296 was violently pillaged from Scotland in the false hope that it would be the symbol of their humiliation and conquest.

That the stone was kept in Westminster Abbey in defiance of a royal command and despite the promise of its return to Scotland.

That by no other means than the forceful removal of the stone from Westminster Abbey was it possible even to secure discussion as to its rightful resting place.

That it is the earnest hope of his Majesty's Scottish people that arrangements for the proper disposition of the stone may now be made after consultation with the General Assembly of the Church of Scotland who as successors of the Abbots of Scone are its natural guardians.

That it is the earnest prayer of his Majesty's loyal subjects who have served his Majesty both in peace and war that the blessing of Almighty God be with the King and all his peoples so that in peace they may enjoy the freedom which sustains the loyalty of affection rather than the obedience of servility. God save the King.

The letter which was addressed to the General Assembly of the Church of Scotland asked that the representatives of the Church should 'speak for the whole people' and arrange with the authorities in England for the Stone of Destiny to be 'retained in Scotland'.

Having witnessed the incredible scene, Wishart described how the stone had been carried on a wooden 'litter' up the former nave of the abbey between the ruins of pillars, to be placed at its symbolic resting place. The abbey's custodian told reporters: 'They laid it at the three stones which marked the site of the high altar. They carried the stone in a reverent manner, their heads were uncovered, and it was a solemn and impressive little ceremony. The men shook hands with me and wished me the best of luck and then went. As soon as I knew that the Stone of Destiny had been placed in my charge I locked the gates. I have always told visitors that one day the Stone of Destiny would come to this historic spot and I am glad that my words have come true.'

Details of the trio who carried out the deed were scarce, save for being billed by Wishart as 'young' and 'well set-up lads'. Their vehicle was big and black – that was all there was to go on. But then, the detail was not really the key as this was a heist which was all about the bigger picture.

The relic, also known as the Stone of Scone, was, and is, of huge symbolic importance to nationalists. The Stone of Destiny was linked to St Columba, who was said to have used it as a travelling altar, and the nation's kings had been crowned on the slab, making it part of the country's historic tapestry. That was until 1299, when King Edward I stormed Scone Abbey and stole it, carrying it off to Westminster Abbey. The history was one which lived fresh in the minds of nationalists.

It remained in London, hidden beneath the Coronation Chair – the oldest piece of furniture in the abbey and one which had been used for 27 coronations up to that point. Only once did the stone ever leave the abbey and that was as far back as 1657 when it was taken across to Westminster Hall for the installation of Cromwell as Lord Protector.

And then came 1950 and a major police incident which saw roadblocks thrown up and some of the country's most senior detectives enlisted. It began when the alarm was raised in the early hours of Christmas morning. The Stone of Destiny was gone and, according to police, there was 'absolutely no trace' of it as they began their search. It was nightwatchman Andrew Hislop who was the first on the scene. He had been doing his rounds when he spotted marks on the altar carpet, indicating that something heavy had been dragged down the stairs and towards a side door. It did not take him long to identify the missing piece and a frantic call to police followed soon after.

The early theory was that those responsible for the heist must have camped out in a chapel at the abbey overnight before springing into action but that proved not to be the case. Closer inspection identified the point of entry, with a wooden door showing signs of having been forced open. It appeared as though a crowbar had been wedged between the door and frame, with significant force needed to then burst it open. Despite the undoubted noise and commotion that would have created, the size of the Westminster buildings meant, through good fortune, the intruders did not arouse suspicion.

That was just the first step for those who had gained entry. A rail which separated the public, in ordinary circumstances, from the Coronation Chair had been pushed away but removing it from the seat was not straightforward. A bar of wood holding the slab in place was peeled away and left splintered in the process. Even then, there was work to be done as the stone was eased out of the confined space where it was held within the chair. A metal plaque, bearing the legend 'Coronation Chair and Stone', was also missing. With the historic piece dislodged, the group then had to manoeuvre it out of the building. The sandstone-coloured artefact was not huge – measuring 26in by 16in by 11in with two rings set into it – but it was heavy and, therefore, cumbersome. Police presumed it had been transferred into a waiting car outside the door at Poets' Corner.

That car, according to early information collated from witness statements, was a Ford Anglia. Descriptions of the vehicle, which was seen in the area at the time of the heist, were issued along with information on a man and woman, both with Scottish accents, who were travelling in it. The assumption was that they were nationalists who were intent on taking the stone back to Scotland with them.

For three months the investigation drew a complete blank. Broadly speaking, the police knew who had stolen it but a list of suspects spanning half the Scottish population was not a great asset to them and narrowing that search proved to be a frustrating effort. They did get within touching distance, as the net closed in on the quartet who had masterminded the headline-grabbing heist. Those individuals were Ian Hamilton, Gavin Vernon, Alan Stuart and Kay Matheson.

Police searched properties across Scotland as they attempted to track down the stone, going as far afield as the Wester Ross croft of Matheson's family. She had been studying at the University of Glasgow when she joined the idealistic gang and stood up to fierce interrogation at the hands of determined officers. She had also been responsible for driving the stone through roadblocks and evading detection as it made its potentially hazardous trip back home. It transpired the stone had broken during its repatriation but it had, in fact, survived far worse in the past, having been targeted once before, in 1914, when a bomb was placed under the Coronation Chair in an attack believed to have been led by the suffragettes.

Months passed before the time was deemed right to take it on the final journey, to Angus. Following its 'delivery' to Arbroath Abbey and subsequent collection by police in April 1951, it was returned to Westminster by the authorities. In 1996 it was returned to Scotland as a gesture of goodwill and can now be seen at Edinburgh Castle. In the 1920s, MP David Kirkwood was given permission to bring a bill for the removal of the stone to the Palace of Holyroodhouse but that bid did not come to fruition.

Even after their identities had become clear, none of the four cross-border raiders faced prosecution. It has been claimed the government feared the student population would rise up and revolt if their varsity counterparts were hauled before the courts.

The death of Matheson in 2013, by then living a quiet life in the Highland village of Aultbea after carving out a reputation as a respected Gaelic scholar and fine teacher, brought the incredible story back to the fore – not that it has ever been far from the Scottish consciousness, having been immortalised by various filmmakers over the years.

The 2008 movie *Stone of Destiny*, in which Matheson's role

was played by Kate Mara, was just one of a number of film and television productions to have touched on the drama of the episode.

Former Liberal Democrat party leader Charles Kennedy was at one stage a fierce political rival of Matheson, as the pair went head to head in elections, but he was among the first to lead the tributes when news of her death broke. Kennedy said she was 'an inspirational force' and added: 'The redoubtable Kay was a truly remarkable character, one of whom I was truly fond and someone who was tremendously kind towards me. I was apprehensive in the extreme when I first stood locally in 1983 to find Kay – of Stone of Destiny fame – as my SNP opponent. In fact we hit it off so well that a firm friendship was formed.'

Ian Hamilton, who went on to qualify in law and rose to serve as Queen's Counsel, has no regrets about his part. Now in his 80s, he told *Telegraph* journalist Olga Craig that the incident remains a source of great pride to him. During that interview in 2008, Hamilton said: 'You sort of know that when you take a crowbar to a side door of Westminster Abbey and jemmy the lock that there isn't really any going back, don't you? Not when you know that the next thing you are going to do is steal one of the ancient relics inside. Not that it was stealing. It was a liberation. A returning of a venerable relic to its rightful ownership. Of course back then I didn't realise the scale of the thing. That it would become an international incident.'

For years Hamilton did not speak about his past – after all, in the years which followed, his life was upholding the law of the land. With age, he relaxed and revealed more about the planning and execution of the heist, giving his approval to the 2008 film version of the story. Directed by Charles Martin Smith, the movie retold the story for a modern audience. It starred Robert Carlyle, a fittingly Scottish casting, and received decent reviews when it aired. Initially, the team behind the concept had hoped to attract Hollywood interest but found the tale of the fight for Scottish independence did not hold much sway in California. In time, funding was secured, with a combination of Scottish and Canadian backers bankrolling the production, and the filming could begin. Beneath the title ran the tag line, 'A heist 600 years in the making'.

Despite enjoying the cinematic re-creation, Hamilton insisted, at the time of the movie's release, that his days as a political activist were long gone. He said: 'No more breaking and entering for me. 'I'm no longer a particularly political person. I believe deeply in my country. But as we say here: "No Scotland, no me". I'm no hero, the title doesn't fit. Yes, though, I am immensely proud that that young man is me.

'I'm not ashamed. In fact I'm rather proud. We drove down the bleak, narrow roads to London to hurt no one. Rather to puncture England's pride. To save no one but the ruined hopes of our country. I wanted to waken the Scots up, that was all.'

It transpired that the then SNP activist John MacCormick had bankrolled the expedition. Bankrolled is perhaps over-glamorising the process – a crisp £50-note was the extent of the financial transaction behind the great heist. That money helped pay for petrol for two cars to make the long and arduous trip on 1950s roads from Glasgow down to the Big Smoke in winter weather and with no heaters. It was not a walk in the park.

They did their homework on the abbey, making an earlier visit and discovering that a door at the east end of the building was made of pine rather than oak. That was the chosen point of entry and it worked a treat. Getting in was only half the battle; the removal element proved more of a challenge than had been expected. Matheson, the getaway driver, waited patiently outside whilst her three partners in crime wrestled with the stone inside. It toppled and smashed in the process, breaking a couple of Scottish toes along the way.

As one piece was transferred to Matheson's car, the plan came unstuck – a policeman, walking the beat, appeared on the scene. Ian Hamilton eloquently documented his experiences in his 1952 book *No Stone Unturned*. In an illuminating passage on the moment the plot almost unravelled, he documented his fear caused by Matheson's decision to move the getaway car into position before the stone was ready to be loaded. Hamilton wrote:

I opened the door, and as I did so I heard the car start up. It moved forward into the lane, whence it was clearly visible from the road. We still had to drag the Stone down the masons' yard. It was far too early to move forward yet. 'The fool,' I said, and dashed through the line of sheds to tell Kay to get back into cover. The car was standing outside the gap in the hoarding. I opened the car door. 'Get the damned car back into cover,' I spat. 'We're not ready yet.'

Kay looked at me coolly. 'A policeman has seen me,' she said. 'He's coming across the road'. I got into the car beside her and silently closed the door. I reached forward, and switched on the lights. I fought breath into myself and wiped the dust of the Abbey off my hands on to Kay's coat. I put one hand over the back of the seat, and groped for Alan's spare coat. Carefully I draped it over the fragment of the Stone. Then I took her in my arms.

It was a strange situation in which we found ourselves, yet neither of us felt perturbed. Kay was as cool and calm, as though we were on our way home from a dance, and for a couple of minutes I was so immersed in the task at hand that I completely forgot the approach of the policeman. It was our third night without sleep, and I think we were both so drugged with tiredness that we would have accepted any situation as normal. Our minds were cold as ice, and we had thrashed our bodies so hard and worked for so long in the shadow of our ultimate aim that fear or panic played no part with us.

The policeman loomed up in front of us. 'What's going on here?' he thundered. It was perfectly obvious what was going on. Kay and I did not fall apart until he had had plenty of opportunity to see us. 'It's Christmas Eve, you know, officer,' I explained. Christmas Eve be damned!' he answered. 'It's five o'clock on Christmas morning.' 'Ochone! Ochone!' I said. 'Is it that time already?'

You're sitting on private property here,' he told us. 'And why did you move forward when you saw me coming?' 'I know,' I said humbly. 'I knew we shouldn't be here. We put on the lights to show you that we were quite willing to move on.'

But where can we go?' asked Kay, vamping him. 'The streets are far too busy.' 'You should be off home,' he told her, and looked at her severely. We explained to him that we were down from Scotland on tour, and that we had arrived in London too late to get a bed. We sat and held hands in front of him, and tried to give him the impression that we were too much in love to go to a hotel and be parted.

He began to warm to us. To my horror, he took off his helmet, and laid it on the roof of the car. He lit a cigarette and showed every sign of staying, till he had smoked it. 'There's a dark car park just along the road,' he said, smacking his lips contemplatively. We knew that car park. The other car was there.

'Och, well,' said Kay, thrusting her head into the lion's mouth, 'if we're not comfortable there we can always get you to run us in and give us a bed in the cells.' 'No! No!' said the PC knowingly. 'There's not a policeman in London would arrest you tonight. None of them want to appear in court on Boxing Day to give evidence against you.' Kay gave my hand a squeeze. 'A good night for crime!' I said, and we all laughed.

All this time I had been conscious of a scraping going on behind the hoarding. Why on earth didn't they lie low until the policeman had gone? It transpired afterwards that they had no idea that we were entertaining the police, and they were calling my parentage in question to the tenth generation for sitting in the car while they did all the work.

Kay heard the noise, too, and we engaged the constable in furious conversation. He thought us excellent company. His slightest sally brought forth peals of laughter, and when he essayed a joke we nearly had convulsions. Surely they would hear our laughter and be warned.

There was a muffled thud from behind the hoarding. The constable stopped speaking, tensed, listening. My heart sank to my boots. Kay's hand became rigid in mine. Then the constable laughed and said, 'That was the old watchman falling down the stairs.' Furiously and hysterically, Kay and I laughed at the idea of the watchman falling down the stairs. Surely they had heard us now. 'I wish it was six o'clock,' said the policeman. 'And then I would be off duty.'

Out of the corner of my eye, I saw the door in the hoarding slowly opening. Gavin's face appeared, followed by his head and shoulders. Suddenly he froze. He had seen the policeman. His lips formed an amazed oath. Inch by inch he edged back, and the door closed behind him. The policeman finished his cigarette and put on his helmet. 'You'd better be going now,' he said. 'We had indeed!' I said, wiping the sweat out of my eyes. 'Will you show us the way?' asked Kay, trying to get him off the premises. 'Oh, you can't miss the car park,' he said, and redirected us.

Kay started the engine. She is, although she will be annoyed that I say so, a very bad driver, but that morning her bad driving was designed and not incompetence. Never has clutch been let in so jerkily; never has a car veered from side to side so crazily. I looked back and waved to the constable. As Kay had expected, he was following down behind us – too amazed at the crazy driving to pay attention to anything else. We reached Old Palace Yard and Kay put her toe down.

Hamilton and his sidekick had managed to talk their way out of the situation but Matheson had no option but to pull away and head for the hills. She drove to Birmingham for the first stop on the journey back, with the remaining three dealing with the other half of the stone. In a delightful detail, the slab was doused in whisky at the border to mark its homecoming.

Of course, it was soon winging its way back south after being reclaimed for Westminster in 1951. Upon its return to Scotland in 1996, it became a popular visitor attraction at Edinburgh Castle – a talking point for tens of thousands who passed through the doors each year.

But the many twists and turns in the story of the Stone of Destiny did not end in 1996. According to many, the greatest mystery remains to be solved.

Two popular theories have been floated. One is that the

English never had the real stone in the first place – that King Edward was duped in 1296 by a replica and canny Scots had squirrelled the real version away to prevent it falling into enemy hands. The other conspiracy tale is that, even if the original had been housed in Westminster, it was not handed back in 1951. The story, whether fact or fiction, is that, when it was liberated by the student quartet, it was hidden away and a very well-made copy was what was ceremonially presented at Arbroath Abbey.

That is a chain of events supported by the family of Bertie Gray, the stonemason who was said to be behind the switch. It was Gray who was entrusted with the difficult job of repairing the stone following the damage inflicted upon it during its liberation from Westminster. According to his children, he made two perfect replicas at the same time – complete with bolts where the repair had been made – and they are convinced the real one was not handed over to the authorities. The intention, it is claimed, was to wait for the hullabaloo to subside and then go public with the facts about the real deal.

But they say their father took the truth to the grave with him when he died in 1975 and even they have been left to fill in the blanks. In the age of modern analysis, it would be possible to forensically examine the stone on show in Edinburgh but then that would spoil the fun. The great charm of the Stone of Destiny is the air of intrigue relating to every facet of its history. Claims, counter-claims and opinion have ensured that almost everyone in the country has their own thoughts on the subject – particularly those of a nationalist leaning.

In 2014, the year in which Alex Salmond, as First Minister, would take his dream of independence for Scotland to a public vote, it is fitting that he has the final word. Salmond said: 'There are two questions that are key to the mystery of the stone. Did the Abbot of Scone meekly surrender Scotland's most famous symbol to Edward in 1296, or did he allow him to ransack a substitute? Was it the real Stone of Destiny that turned up on the altar at Arbroath Abbey in 1951 after being repatriated by Ian Hamilton and friends, or was it a replica made by bailie

Bertie Gray? On balance, my view is that the Abbot of Scone furnished Edward with a substitute. What I believe cannot be in doubt is that the stone currently in Edinburgh Castle is the one that lay in Westminster Abbey for 700 years. Neither question can ever be finally answered – and that is why the mystery of the stone is one best left unsolved.'

Postscript

The extraordinary lengths the figures behind some of Scotland's biggest heists have gone to have been well documented in the pages of this book. What has only been touched upon in passing is the answer to a very simple question: why?

Why have so many people taken it upon themselves to kill, torture, threaten and plot to get their hands on other people's money and possessions? And remember, the cases featured in this book are only a tiny proportion of the raids and robberies conducted in Scotland in modern times. Many, many more have been carried out with varying results.

It would be wrong to suggest there is one underlying factor running through the cases outlined – each was very different – but, when boiled down and analysed, there is a clutch of common motives behind these incredible crimes and many of those have been outlined by those who know best – the raiders themselves. At various stages, usually during court proceedings, pleas of mitigation have been made and the driving forces behind particular episodes have been relayed either in person or by legal counsel. Some appear more plausible than others but most have been repeated at one stage or another during the course of completely unrelated cases.

The first of those is quite simple – desperation. The need to access large sums of money quickly may seem an obvious motivation but, in fact, a 'desperate' need is only occasionally cited. In the case of Howard Wilson, the policeman who turned armed robber and murderer, it was, of course, business troubles, leading to debt, which prompted his move into a new and illicit line of work. In more recent times, for example in the failed ram raid on the HSBC premises in Lanarkshire, the same explanation was offered up. And, in the case of the Bowers brothers, their crimes were said to have been prompted by a desire to save their gym business.

Desperation can take many forms and addiction is part of that problem, as demonstrated by the Perth museum thefts which saw ancient coins sold off for a fraction of their true worth as a means to service the culprit's heroin dependency. Albeit on a different scale to the type of major heists featured in this book, a brief glimpse at any newspaper on any given day will tell the story of the frequency of armed raids and robberies for relatively small returns by addicts in need of quick and convenient cash.

Of course, greed is another of the big motivators for those with a mind to pull off major heists. There was no suggestion that Alexander Gray, a bookmaker and apparently successful gambling club operator, desperately *needed* cash when he pulled together the team required to pull off the 'Plasticine' robbery at Shettleston bank but he did desperately *want* that money.

The same could be said of those behind the black market which supports the art and antiquities thefts which have left many innocent people heartbroken and have deprived the public of some significant works. Those who target rhino horn to profit from its medicinal uses are interested purely in the proceeds, not in the heritage and culture behind it. Those who stole the Leonardo da Vinci masterpiece *The Madonna of the Yarnwinder* from Drumlanrig Castle had pound signs in their eyes, not any concern for the owner who was left devastated by its disappearance and who died before it had been safely found and recovered, thankfully, having escaped any damage during the regrettable incident.

The influence of a criminal lifestyle has undoubtedly been a major contributing factor to many cases too. Going right back to 1806 and the murder of William Begbie, if James Mackcoull was indeed the killer, all of the evidence suggests the robbery was just the latest in a long line of crimes which has become a way of life for the Londoner. Whether picking pockets, robbing banks or slaying innocent people he saw it purely as a means to an end. It is what a habit that he couldn't, or perhaps wouldn't, shake.

In more recent times, the heist from the Asda store at The Jewel in Edinburgh was another which appeared to be born from a trend in the underworld. Ram-raiding was a 1990s phenomenon and that particular version of the criminal trend simply took it to a whole new level. There was clear evidence to suggest that the passion for ram-raiding was spreading through criminal gangs in certain parts of the country, the north of England being a hotspot, and it demonstrated the almost contagious nature some types of crime can have. It was no surprise to many in law enforcement circles when it transpired that those suspected of the raid on the store in Scotland's capital originated from what at the time was the ram-raiding capital of England – Newcastle.

Every now again, an example of a very unusual motive comes along and the act prompted by that motive gives its perpetrators the chance to make a statement. The story behind the Stone of Destiny demonstrated that – not least because those responsible had no intention of keeping their 'loot'. Instead, they hand-delivered it back to the authorities in a manner which was guaranteed to grab headlines and gain vital exposure for their nationalist cause. It was an intricate plot by intelligent people and it served its purpose well. The very fact it is still being spoken and written about more than 60 years on is testament to that. Could the Stone of Destiny theft be the one crime examined here that is, indeed, victimless? After all, nationalists would argue that it was already stolen property when it was installed in Westminster Abbey in the first place – according to their own claim, they were simply taking back what was already theirs.

In virtually every other crime detailed in these pages, there was a very real victim – in some cases, they paid the ultimate price, losing their life for no other reason that they stood between a thief and their chosen haul. In anyone's eyes, the use of such force and terror can never be justified. And who could claim the trauma caused for victims of an armed raid could be worthwhile simply to satisfy a craving? Bizarrely, among a certain section of the criminal fraternity, that craving is, indeed, the overwhelming motive behind their life of crime. It sounds incredible but some who have indulged in the dark arts of the armed robbery have cited the thrill generated by being in the midst of a major heist as their incentive.

James Crosbie is held up as one of the most obvious and best-known examples for whom this was true. He had success in business but still he went back to what he knew best – robbing banks. Crosbie had the type of life many of his peers growing up in Glasgow could only have dreamt of. He earned his pilot's licence and experienced life in Africa during some of his many adventures but it wasn't enough. Nothing could replicate the buzz he got from planning and executing the armed robberies which made him infamous. Even today, with his life on a different path, he is known for his books chronicling the types of episodes which landed him in prison.

This was, after all, the man who made one of his getaway dashes by bicycle – not because he had to but because he could. He thought about it, set the plan in motion and then carried it through to see if it would succeed. And it did – he pedalled away with the cash from his latest bank job in a rucksack and left police trailing in his wake. It was the type of game of cat and mouse that Crosbie appeared to thrive on although, ultimately, it ended in defeat as he was convicted and jailed. Perhaps in his mind that was just one of the results of the game he played – nothing ventured, nothing gained.

In so much as he turned it into a profitable enterprise for a period of time, Crosbie, in some ways, could be seen as successful in what he did. Much of the cash stolen was never recovered and, for large periods during his criminal career, he remained at large and able to enjoy the fruits of his efforts.

Others were less proficient but were driven by a similar craving that Crosbie had demonstrated throughout his life. That has been exemplified by a man not featured in the preceding 16 chapters but with a story worth recounting now as the motivations for those responsible for some of Scotland's heists are chewed over.

His name is Paul Macklin, and late in 2013 he walked free from prison after serving eight years in prison following an attempted £300,000 payroll robbery. Macklin was not desperate for money. He was not that concerned about the potential profit from his plot so could not be considered to be acting purely through greed. He was not steeped in a criminal lifestyle – far from it – and nor was he in any way trying to make a statement. What he did have was a craving for the adrenaline rush that, in his mind, only an armed robbery could bring.

To put his actions in context, it should be explained that Macklin came from a privileged background. His father was a high-flying executive in the booming multi-billion-pound North Sea oil industry and, as such, could afford the finer things in life for his son. That included the type of education that only plenty of money can buy. Macklin spent most of his latter school years at the prestigious Gordonstoun School in Moray. Its sprawling 200-acre campus, amid rolling glens and scenic woodland, is an idyllic location in which to live and learn. Macklin followed in the footsteps of royalty, with Prince Charles among the best-known alumni of the boarding establishment. Prince Phillip too was a former pupil so it was little surprise that Charles and his brothers, Prince Andrew and Prince Edward, were also enrolled there.

The school attracts pupils from all over the world and promotes what is described as a 'fully inclusive' educational programme based on the four distinct educational principles of 'Challenge, Service, Internationalism and Responsibility'. Parents are promised that students will be 'challenged academically, physically and emotionally' and told that the opportunities available to pupils provide them with 'significant life-shaping experiences'. But it was whilst growing up as a Gordonstoun pupil that Macklin claims the seeds for his criminal future were first sown, as he opted not to follow the traditional path of his contemporaries and pursue a career in the familiar fields of finance, law and medicine. He had different plans and they did not involve conformity in any shape or form.

By the age of 21 he was preparing for life behind bars. That was his punishment for a failed heist in 1994 in which he and Robert Cadiz, another former public school pupil, attempted to raid an Aberdeen City Council depot in the city's Kittybrewster district. They were armed with guns and wire cutters as they chased the potential reward of a £300,000 haul – cash intended to pay wages. But Macklin and Cadiz did not net a single penny, despite months of planning.

The pair had met at Robert Gordon's College in Aberdeen, the fee-paying school Macklin attended after being expelled from Gordonstoun during his fifth-year studies. Its FP list reads like a sporting *Who's Who*, with everything from Olympic gold medal winners to Scotland rugby stars, not to mention a plethora of old boys who have gone on to make it big in business. Macklin and Cadiz were not the archetypal Gordon's boys and had their hearts set on different achievements, if you can use that term. But, before they had carried out their big-money plot, they were stopped and searched by police who discovered a pump-action shotgun in one of their holdalls. They threatened officers with what was believed to be a gun in their other bag before making off on foot and then hijacking a passing car to continue their getaway.

The duo were later arrested and, despite a legal fight, Macklin was sentenced to eight years in jail for his part in the attempted robbery and for threatening four police officers and the motorist. Cadiz received a three-year sentence but was also jailed for six years for an armed robbery on a branch of the Clydesdale Bank in an Aberdeen suburb. On that occasion, he had acted with an accomplice but steadfastly refused to name that individual.

After being released from his first sentence, having served six years, Macklin was jailed again when he was found guilty of threatening police officers with a gun during an incident in 2003. It followed a robbery on a property used as a safe house by drug dealers in the Printfield area of Aberdeen – a crime he maintains to this day he was not involved in. Macklin, upon his release from prison in 2013, vowed to clear his name by challenging his most recent conviction in the Supreme Court.

Now in his 40s, he also took the opportunity to talk at length about the reason for his initial armed raid plans. In an interview with the *Press and Journal* newspaper, Macklin said: 'It is almost embarrassing to say this now, but when I was 18 I was into adrenalin and extreme sports – skiing, gliding, sky-diving, bungee jumping. Then I saw *Point Break*, which presents an armed robbery like an extreme sport. I thought to myself: "I'm going to have a bit of this". It was kind of an adrenalin thing doing these robberies, at the time I was only concerned with my own selfish motivations.'

Point Break is the 1991 Hollywood blockbuster starring Keanu Reeves and Patrick Swayze. Swayze plays the role of the leader of a gang of surfers who, as a profitable sideline, have been pulling off a string of armed robberies and are pursued by the FBI. It was something of a film icon in its era and, despite Macklin's protestations of embarrassment, it is not difficult to see the connection between glamorous big-screen portrayals and the actions of impressionable individuals.

The cinema industry has been arguably the biggest beneficiary of heists through the years with many box-office hits being born from the true-crime genre. From the 1955 film-noir movie *Rififi* to mainstream offerings such as *The Italian Job*, *Ocean's Eleven* and *Lock Stock and Two Smoking Barrels*, there has never been a shortage of offerings which have glamorised the heist. There is no denying that there is something enthralling and captivating about the plots of such films. The planning, clockwork precision, elaborate execution and the suspense of the getaway have all been captured in glorious Technicolor to be enjoyed by audiences intent on two hours of escapism. If you have picked up this book, the chances are you, like me, will have enjoyed at least some of those films. What the research and writing involved in this project has reinforced is that the fiction is far more palatable than the brutal, honest truth.

Patrick Swayze and Keanu Reeves were chosen for roles in *Point Break* to add glamour to the story and the same is also true of George Clooney, Brad Pitt and Matt Damon in *Ocean's Eleven* and Mark Wahlberg in the 2003 remake of *The Italian Job*. It is fair to say that Scotland's real-life equivalents were not cut from the same cloth as their Hollywood counterparts and their airbrushed versions of the epic heists but many chased the rush that has been portrayed so often in the movies. Macklin was one of those and, to this day, he insists he does not wish he had ignored his urge to attempt to rob the Kittybrewster depot, believing it was all part of growing up for him. He said: 'I was 21 years old and I took a shot at hundreds of thousands of pounds. To have missed the years 21 to 26 was not the end of the world. If there are people out there who I have hurt, I definitely regret any part in that and I apologise.'

Macklin outlined his hope to indulge his love of skiing by finding employment on the slopes of the French Alps, clearly hoping a new life abroad will allow him to put his chequered past behind him. He was not perturbed by his experiences in the prison system either and, in fact, he claimed: 'I never found prison particularly hard. It was just like Gordonstoun. I remember one disgraced aristocrat, who had been to Eton, was asked how he survived when he came home from prison. He said that any man who had been to a public school or in the Army will be quite at home. For me, that's how it was.'

Speaking of his time at Gordonstoun, he added: 'You are living there eight months a year with around 50 to 60 other boys. Obviously, there is not a lot of parental supervision and you have a culture of 13- to 18-year-olds who live among themselves and police themselves. It creates a very independent child from an early age.'

It should be stressed that the principal of Gordonstoun was quick to denounce those claims, stating: 'We do not recognise the school that Paul Macklin is describing. Pastoral care is highly structured at Gordonstoun and is at the heart of everything we do. Gordonstoun works hard to make sure a culture

Hertfordshire Libraries

Watford Central Library
Kiosk 2

Customer ID: *****2030

Items that you have borrowed

Title: Heist : the inside story of
   Scotland's most notorious
Due: 23 July 2022

Title: Hertfordshire murders
Due: 23 July 2022

   Items: 2
   t outstanding: £0 00
   loan: 2
      0
   ns: 0
      llection: 0
      :38

   ing Hertfordshire

   als go to
   .gov.uk/libraries
   23 4049

of mutual support and kindness is fostered in every member of the school community.'

What Macklin's life of wealth and opportunity proves is that there is no stereotypical perpetrator. Each heist will have its own story, with peculiarities and twists in the tale. Prevention will always be better than the cure but curbing the plentiful motivating factors will, in reality, be impossible.

There will always be desperation, greed, criminal lifestyles, people intent on making political statements and those who crave the thrill of the chase. The challenge facing businesses, individuals and the police is to be ready and waiting to ensure those who do choose to travel that path are met with the steely resistance which has thwarted so many attempts in the past.

Bibliography

NEWSPAPER ARCHIVES
Press and Journal
Evening Express
The Scotsman
Glasgow Herald
Evening Times
Bulletin (Glasgow)
Daily Record
Sunday Mail
Southern Reporter
Greenock Telegraph

ONLINE ARCHIVES AND RESOURCES
National Library of Scotland
STV
BBC
www.safeman.org.uk
www.arthostage.blogspot.com
www.secretscotland.org.uk
www.professionaljeweller.com
www.g4s.uk.com

OTHER SOURCES
The Public Ledger
Trafficking Culture, research report, Glasgow University/
    Dr Simon Mackenzie et al
Ashanti Gold, James Crosbie (Black and White Publishing)
The Stone of Destiny, Ian Hamilton (Birlinn)